BBC goodfood

SOUPS & SIDES

20 19 18 17 16 15 14

BBC Books, an imprint of Ebury Publishing
20 Vauxhall Bridge Road,
London SW1V 2SA

BBC Books is part of the Penguin Random House
group of companies whose addresses can
be found at global.penguinrandomhouse.com

Penguin
Random House
UK

Photographs © BBC Magazines 2010
Recipes © BBC Magazines 2010
Book design © Woodlands Books Ltd 2010
All recipes contained in this book first
appeared in BBC *Good Food* magazine.

First published by BBC Books in 2010

www.eburypublishing.co.uk

A CIP catalogue record for this book
is available from the British Library

ISBN 9781846079160

Printed and bound in China by Toppan Leefung

Commissioning Editor: Muna Reyal
Project Editor: Joe Cottington
Designer: Annette Peppis
Production: Lucy Harrison
Picture Researcher: Gabby Harrington
Cover Design: Interstate Creative Partners Ltd

Penguin Random House is committed
to a sustainable future for our business, our
readers and our planet. This book is made from
Forest Stewardship Council® certified paper.

FSC
www.fsc.org

MIX
Paper from
responsible sources
FSC® C018179

PICTURE CREDITS

BBC *Good Food* magazine and BBC Books
would like to thank the following people for
providing photos. While every effort has
been made to trace and acknowledge all
photographers, we should like to apologise
should there be any errors or omissions.

Chris Alack p41, p89; Clive Bozzard-Hill p105;
Simon Brown p101; Peter Cassidy p139, p149,
p153, p181, p205; Jean Cazals p25, p73, p83,
p85; Ken Field p53, p55, p93, p95, p97;
Dean Grennan p159; Will Heap p11, p67;
Jonathan Krause p87, p133; William Lingwood
p99; Gareth Morgans p21, p31, p47, p121, p129,
p141, p161, p163, p185, p199, p201, p207;
David Munns p15, p29, p33, p59, p61, p69, p71,
p135, p137, p157, p165, p187; Noel Murphy p63;
Sean Myers p19, p27; Myles New p23, p37, p39,
p45, p49, p57, p117, p119, p123, p147, p183, p189,
p191, p197, p203, 211; Elisabeth Parsons p17, p65,
p77, p79, p107, p109, p113, p115, p127, p151, p155,
p175, p177, p179, p193, p195; Craig Robertson
p35; Roger Stowell p111; Yuki Sugiura p125, p169;
Adrian Taylor p171; Debi Treloar p103; Ian Wallace
p91; Simon Walton p75, p173; Philip Webb p13,
p43, p51, p143, p145, p209; Kate Whitaker p81;
Elizabeth Zeschin p167

All the recipes in this book were created
by the editorial team at *Good Food* and
by regular contributors to BBC Magazines.

good food
SOUPS & SIDES

EDITOR
Sharon Brown

BOOKS

Contents

Introduction 6

Speedy soups
10

Low-fat ideas
44

Hearty favourites
78

Special soups for
entertaining   112

Tasty sides
146

Lunchtime snacks
178

Index 212

Introduction

A delicious soup really fits the bill for so many occasions – a light lunch, a main meal supper, a tempting starter, and a take-to-school treat in a flask. It's also the ultimate comfort food, for what could be better on a chilly day than a warming bowlful of goodness?

Soups are easy to make, too; chopped vegetables simmered in a good stock and then whizzed in a food processor to a smooth finish is the simple method for most soups. Packed with protein and vitamin-enriched veg, soups are a great way to achieve your 5-a-day and an excellent idea for getting children to eat more of those good-for-you veg.

Soups are a good idea for the thrifty cook, as you can make the most of seasonal and local veg when it's a bargain buy, so check out farmers' markets and farm shops. Plus don't forget you can use up the leftovers in the vegetable drawer – simply pop them straight into your next soup and don't let those lovely flavours go to waste!

We've also included a collection of tasty sides – all great served with soup or on their own. There are simple-make scones, breads and wraps and some mouth-watering snacks like *Baked garlic mushrooms*, *Smoked mackerel dip* and *Summer sausage rolls*.

Here are 101 favourites for you to cook and enjoy from the *Good Food* kitchen – all with our famous triple-tested guarantee so you can cook with confidence first time.

Sharon

Sharon Brown
Good Food magazine

Notes and conversion tables

NOTES ON THE RECIPES
- Eggs are large in the UK and Australia and extra large in America unless stated otherwise.
- Wash fresh produce before preparation.
- Recipes contain nutritional analyses for 'sugar', which means the total sugar content including all natural sugars in the ingredients, unless otherwise stated.

OVEN TEMPERATURES

Gas	°C	°C Fan	°F	Oven temp.
¼	110	90	225	Very cool
½	120	100	250	Very cool
1	140	120	275	Cool or slow
2	150	130	300	Cool or slow
3	160	140	325	Warm
4	180	160	350	Moderate
5	190	170	375	Moderately hot
6	200	180	400	Fairly hot
7	220	200	425	Hot
8	230	210	450	Very hot
9	240	220	475	Very hot

APPROXIMATE WEIGHT CONVERSIONS
- All the recipes in this book list both imperial and metric measurements. Conversions are approximate and have been rounded up or down. Follow one set of measurements only; do not mix the two.
- Cup measurements, which are used by cooks in Australia and America, have not been listed here as they vary from ingredient to ingredient. Kitchen scales should be used to measure dry/solid ingredients.

Good Food is concerned about sustainable sourcing and animal welfare. Where possible, humanely reared meats, sustainably caught fish (see fishonline.org for further information from the Marine Conservation Society) and free-range chickens and eggs are used when recipes are originally tested.

SPOON MEASURES

Spoon measurements are level unless otherwise specified.

- 1 teaspoon (tsp) = 5ml
- 1 tablespoon (tbsp) = 15ml
- 1 Australian tablespoon = 20ml (cooks in Australia should measure 3 teaspoons where 1 tablespoon is specified in a recipe)

APPROXIMATE LIQUID CONVERSIONS

metric	imperial	AUS	US
50ml	2fl oz	¼ cup	¼ cup
125ml	4fl oz	½ cup	½ cup
175ml	6fl oz	¾ cup	¾ cup
225ml	8fl oz	1 cup	1 cup
300ml	10fl oz/½ pint	½ pint	1¼ cups
450ml	16fl oz	2 cups	2 cups/1 pint
600ml	20fl oz/1 pint	1 pint	2½ cups
1 litre	35fl oz/1¾ pints	1¾ pints	1 quart

Smoked haddock chowder

You can make this soup even more special by serving poached eggs on top. Or up your 5-a-day total by slicing two leeks and cooking them with the onion and potatoes.

TAKES 25 MINUTES • SERVES 2

1 onion, chopped
2 potatoes, scrubbed and sliced
500ml/18fl oz vegetable stock
2 smoked haddock fillets, about
   100g/4oz each, skinned and cut
   into chunks
418g can creamed corn
4 tbsp milk, or to taste
handful of parsley leaves, chopped

1 Put the onion and potatoes into a large sauté pan, pour over the stock and simmer for 6–8 minutes until the potatoes are soft but still have a slight bite to them.

2 Add the chunks of smoked haddock, tip in the creamed corn and add the milk – if you like a thinner chowder, add more. Gently simmer for 5–7 minutes until the haddock is cooked (it should flake easily when pressed with a fork). Ladle into bowls and sprinkle over the chopped parsley to serve.

PER SERVING 555 kcals, protein 37g, carbs 84g, fat 10g, sat fat 3g, fibre 7g, sugar none, salt 0.3g

Pea & watercress soup

Fresh peas and peppery watercress are a perfect match in summer, but you can adapt this soup to eat it year-round – try spring onions, rocket and sorrel in spring.

TAKES 20 MINUTES ● SERVES 4

1 tbsp olive oil
1 onion, finely chopped
1 garlic clove, roughly chopped
1 medium potato, cut into small chunks
500ml/18fl oz vegetable stock
300g/10oz fresh peas (or frozen if out of season)
100g/4oz watercress
leaves from 2 mint sprigs, plus extra to garnish
100ml/3½fl oz double cream

1 Heat the oil in a large pan, then gently fry the onion and garlic for 5 minutes or until soft. Add the potato, stock and 500ml water, then simmer for 7 minutes until the potato is just cooked.
2 Scatter in the peas and watercress, stir, cover, then simmer for 3 minutes. Add the mint leaves and blitz with an electric hand blender until smooth.
3 Stir in the cream and season to taste. Serve ladled into bowls and scatter with more mint and some black pepper.

PER SERVING 256 kcals, protein 8g, carbs 17g, fat 18g, sat fat 8g, fibre 5g, sugar 5g, salt 0.21g

Sweet potato & chickpea soup

This quick-to-make soup is low in fat and salt, and makes a great choice to pour into a Thermos flask for a warming lunch on the move.

TAKES 25 MINUTES • SERVES 2

1 tbsp olive oil
1 onion, finely diced
2 garlic cloves, sliced
1 tsp ground cumin
1 tsp ground coriander
1 sweet potato, peeled and cut into
   1cm/½in cubes
600ml/1 pint hot vegetable stock
220g can chickpeas, drained and rinsed
1 tbsp soured cream
50ml/2fl oz milk

1 Heat the olive oil in a pan, add the onion and cook for 3 minutes until soft. Add the garlic and cook for 3 minutes more. Add the cumin and coriander, and cook for 1 minute.

2 Add the sweet potato and fry for 2 minutes, then pour over the vegetable stock. Boil for 10 minutes until the potato is tender. Add the drained chickpeas and heat through. Whizz in a food processor until smooth. Stir in the soured cream and milk, and serve when hot or pour into a flask to carry to work or school.

PER SERVING 287 kcals, protein 10g, carbs 40g, fat 11g, sat fat 2g, fibre 7g, sugar 12g, salt 0.89g

Prawn & coconut laksa

Cooking for one can be fun when it takes under 20 minutes to make a delicious bowlful of satisfying soup like this one.

TAKES 18 MINUTES • SERVES 1

2 tsp oil
1 garlic clove, crushed
1 spring onion, finely chopped
2 tsp finely chopped ginger
1 green chilli, deseeded and finely
    chopped
juice of ½ lime
100g/4oz raw peeled prawns (any size)
165ml can coconut milk
100ml/3½fl oz chicken or vegetable
    stock
100g/4oz dried egg noodles
chopped coriander leaves, to garnish

1 Heat the oil in a large pan or wok. When hot, throw in the garlic, spring onion, ginger and green chilli. Cook on a medium heat for 3–4 minutes, then squeeze in the lime juice.

2 Stir in the prawns, then add the coconut milk and stock. Simmer gently for 5 minutes on a low heat until the prawns are pink.

3 Meanwhile, cook the egg noodles in a pan of boiling water for 4 minutes until soft. Drain, then tip into the prawn mixture. Season to taste and serve in a bowl, topped with the coriander.

PER SERVING 823 kcals, protein 33g, carbs 79g, fat 44g, sat fat 25g, fibre 3g, sugar 7g, salt 2.19g

Spicy bean soup with avocado salsa

If you like Mexican flavours, this soup is for you. The fresh-tasting salsa topping makes a perfect contrast to the spicy, tomatoey soup.

TAKES 30 MINUTES ● SERVES 4

FOR THE SOUP

1 tbsp olive oil

1 onion, finely chopped

1 garlic clove, crushed

400g can kidney beans in chilli sauce

300ml/½ pint hot vegetable stock

200g can chopped tomatoes

¼ tsp dried chilli flakes

200ml/7fl oz crème fraîche

FOR THE SALSA

1 ripe avocado, finely diced

1 beefsteak tomato, deseeded and finely diced

1 small red onion, finely chopped

15g pack coriander, roughly chopped, plus extra leaves to garnish

1 Heat the oil in a large pan and fry the onion and garlic for 2–3 minutes until softened. Add the kidney beans with their chilli sauce, the stock, tomatoes and chilli flakes. Bring to the boil and simmer for 2–3 minutes.

2 Meanwhile, make the salsa. Put the avocado, tomato, red onion and coriander in a small bowl, mix, and season to taste.

3 Pour the soup into a blender or food processor and process until smooth. Return to the pan and heat through. Add two-thirds of the crème fraîche and reheat without boiling, stirring continuously. Season to taste.

4 Ladle the soup into bowls and top with a spoonful each of the remaining crème fraîche and the salsa. Serve garnished with the coriander leaves.

PER SERVING 341 kcals, protein 11g, carbs 27g, fat 22g, sat fat 8g, fibre 9g, sugar none, salt 1.39g

Spicy coconut noodle soup

This recipe is based on laksa, a traditional Malaysian noodle soup. It can be made with either rice or egg noodles, depending on what you have in the cupboard.

TAKES 15 MINUTES ● SERVES 4

1 tbsp red curry paste

400ml can coconut milk (use reduced-fat if you prefer)

100g pack mixed mushrooms

1 sheet wide rice noodles, soaked according to the packet instructions

100g bag beansprouts

1 fat green chilli, sliced into rings

½ bunch spring onions, finely chopped

1 Heat a pan and fry the curry paste in it for 1 minute. Add the coconut milk and half a can of water, and bring to the boil. Simmer for 5 minutes until slightly thickened.

2 Throw in the mushrooms and simmer for another 2 minutes. Stir in the drained noodles, beansprouts and most of the chilli and spring onions, then heat for another minute. Serve in deep bowls, scattered with the rest of the chilli and spring onions.

PER SERVING 226 kcals, protein 4g, carbs 15g, fat 17g, sat fat 14g, fibre 1g, sugar 4g, salt 0.45g

Speedy sweet potato soup with coconut

This flavoursome low-fat soup has just a hint of Thai curry paste coming through. Serve with warmed mini naan breads for the perfect accompaniment.

TAKES 20 MINUTES ● SERVES 4

1 tbsp vegetable oil
1 onion, chopped
1–2 tsp Thai curry paste, red or green
750g/1lb 10oz sweet potatoes, grated
1 litre/1¾ pints vegetable stock
½ sachet creamed coconut (or use
   ¼ can reduced-fat coconut milk)
handful of coriander leaves, roughly
   chopped
mini naan breads, to serve

1 Heat the oil in a deep pan then soften the onion for 4–5 minutes. Stir in the curry paste and cook for 1 minute more until fragrant. Add the grated sweet potatoes and stock, then bring to the boil quickly, simmering for 5 minutes until the potato is tender.

2 Remove the soup from the heat, stir in the coconut and seasoning, then cool briefly before whizzing with an electric stick blender until smooth. Sprinkle with coriander and serve with warm mini naan breads.

PER SERVING 240 kcals, protein 4g, carbs 45g, fat 6g, sat fat 3g, fibre 6g, sugar 15g, salt 0.56g

Classic asparagus soup

Asparagus has such a short season, so make the most of it with this soup that you can freeze for up to a month. On a warm day, this is also delicious served cold.

TAKES 30 MINUTES • SERVES 4

25g/1oz butter
2 shallots, diced
700g/1lb 9oz asparagus, trimmed,
   stems chopped and tips reserved
850ml/1½ pints fresh chicken stock
olive oil, to drizzle

1 Melt the butter in a pan, add the shallots and asparagus stems, and cook on a medium heat for 5 minutes. Reduce the heat, cook for 5 minutes more, stirring often. Add the stock, bring to a simmer and cook for 5 minutes until the veg has softened, then remove from the heat and cool.

2 Liquidise the soup until smooth. Return to the pan, season, heat gently and keep warm. Cook the asparagus tips in a pan of boiling water for 2 minutes then drain well. Serve the soup topped with the tips and drizzled with olive oil.

PER SERVING 96 kcals, protein 6g, carbs 4g, fat 6g, sat fat 3g, fibre 3g, sugar 4g, salt 1g

Chickpea soup with coriander & lime butter

This is a real welcome-home warmer for a cold day. The chilli adds a spicy heat and the lime gives a zingy hit – a wonderful combination.

TAKES 30 MINUTES ● SERVES 4

50g/2oz butter, softened

2 tbsp chopped coriander leaves, plus extra to garnish

finely grated zest and juice of 1 lime

1 tbsp sunflower oil

1 onion, finely chopped

1 red pepper, deseeded and finely chopped

2 garlic cloves, crushed

2 red chillies, deseeded and thinly sliced

1 tsp each ground coriander and cumin

2 × 410g cans chickpeas, drained and rinsed

1.2 litres/2 pints vegetable stock

warm pitta bread, to serve

1 Cream together the butter, fresh coriander, lime zest and seasoning. Spoon on to greaseproof paper and roll up into a sausage shape. Put the flavoured butter in the freezer.

2 Heat the oil in a pan and fry the onion for 2–3 minutes until softened. Add the pepper, garlic and half the chillies, and cook for 2–3 minutes, stirring. Stir in the ground coriander and cumin, and cook for a further minute.

3 Stir in the chickpeas and stock. Bring to the boil and simmer, uncovered, for 15 minutes. Whizz the soup with an electric hand blender until smooth (or use a food processor) then return the soup to the pan and heat through. Stir in the lime juice and season to taste.

4 Ladle into bowls and top with a slice of the coriander and lime butter, the remaining chilli and extra fresh coriander leaves. Serve with warm pitta bread.

PER SERVING 450 kcals, protein 18g, carbs 39g, fat 26g, sat fat 10g, fibre 10g, sugar none, salt 2.52g.

Minted pea soup

Go for frozen petits pois, if you can find them – they'll give you the sweetest flavour. This is a dead easy soup to make for a starter when you're entertaining.

TAKES 10 MINUTES • SERVES 4

1 bunch spring onions
good knob of butter
300g/10oz frozen minted peas
700ml/1¼ pints hot vegetable stock
3 tbsp crème fraîche

1 Thinly slice the spring onions, reserving some of the green tops for the garnish. Heat the butter in a pan and fry the spring onions for 1 minute until slightly softened. Add the peas and stock, and bring to the boil. Simmer for 5 minutes, then whizz half the soup in a food processor.

2 Return to the pan with the crème fraîche. Reheat gently, taste, and add black pepper and salt if required. Ladle into small bowls, or cups with saucers, then sprinkle with the reserved spring onion tops.

PER SERVING 122 kcals, protein 6g, carbs 8g, fat 7g, sat fat 5g, fibre 4g, sugar 3g, salt 0.67g

Leek & bacon soup with rosemary

Just five ingredients make up this tasty soup – sure to be a favourite with all the family. The addition of pasta turns the soup into a main meal.

TAKES 25 MINUTES ● SERVES 4

4 leeks, trimmed and thickly sliced
8 rashers smoked streaky bacon,
    chopped
1.5 litres/2¾ pints hot chicken stock
2 rosemary sprigs, needles finely
    chopped
200g/8oz pasta shapes
warm toasted ciabatta, to serve

1 Heat a large pan, then fry the leeks and bacon over a medium heat for 5 minutes until the bacon is crisp and the leeks have started to soften. Pour in the stock and stir in the rosemary with some seasoning. Bring to the boil, then simmer for 5 minutes.

2 Tip in the pasta of your choice and continue to cook for about 10 minutes until the pasta is al dente. Serve with warm toasted ciabatta.

PER SERVING 322 kcals, protein 16g, carbs 42g, fat 11g, sat fat 4g, fibre 4g, sugar 4g, salt 2.53g

Fragrant cucumber & yogurt soup

Serve this chilled summer soup with flatbreads – they can be found in most large supermarkets, and they're a tasty and interesting alternative to traditional breads.

TAKES 10 MINUTES, PLUS CHILLING
● **SERVES 4**

2 cucumbers, roughly chopped
500g pot Greek yogurt
300ml carton fresh chicken stock
2 garlic cloves, crushed
handful of mint leaves, plus extra
   to garnish
2 flatbreads
2 tbsp extra-virgin olive oil

1 Put the cucumbers in a food processor with the yogurt, stock, garlic and mint, then season to taste. Blend until smooth, then pour into a jug. Put in the freezer for 20 minutes to chill.

2 When ready to serve, heat the grill. Brush one side of both flatbreads with 2 teaspoons of the oil, and grill for 1 minute or until browned and crisp.

3 To serve, pour the soup into chilled bowls or glasses. Drizzle over the remaining oil, season with a little cracked black pepper and top with the extra mint leaves. Serve with the crisp flatbreads on the side.

PER SERVING 312 kcals, protein 13g, carbs 27g, fat 18g, sat fat 8g, fibre 2g, sugar none, salt 0.9g

Versatile veg soup

Here's a great way to use up those veg lurking in the bottom of the fridge – chop them up and turn them into a delicious soup.

TAKES 25 MINUTES • SERVES 2

200g/8oz vegetables (such as onions, celery and carrots), chopped
300g/10oz potatoes, peeled and cubed
1 tbsp oil
700ml/1¼ pints vegetable stock
crème fraîche and chopped mixed herbs, to garnish

1 Fry the chopped vegetables with the potatoes in the oil for a few minutes until beginning to soften.

2 Cover with the stock and simmer for 10–15 minutes until the vegetables are tender. Blend until smooth, then season. Serve topped with a dollop of crème fraîche and some fresh herbs.

PER SERVING 211 kcals, protein 5g, carbs 35g, fat 7g, sat fat 1g, fibre 5g, sugar 8g, salt 0.95g

Potato & Savoy cabbage soup with bacon

This veg-packed hearty soup is perfect to come home to on a chilly day. The strips of crisp streaky bacon add a tasty topping to the vegetables.

TAKES 20 MINUTES • SERVES 4

1 onion
1 carrot, peeled
1 celery stick
2 garlic cloves
1 tbsp olive oil, plus extra to garnish
550g/1lb 4oz floury potatoes, peeled and cut into small cubes
1 litre/1¾ pints chicken or vegetable stock
8 rashers streaky bacon
¼ medium Savoy cabbage (about 200g/8oz)

1 Chop the onion, carrot, celery and garlic in a food processor. Heat the oil in a large pan over a medium heat. Add the chopped vegetables and the potatoes, season well, then reduce the heat and cover the pan. Gently cook for about 5 minutes until starting to soften, then add the stock, turn up the heat and bring to the boil. Simmer for 5 minutes more or until all the vegetables are tender.

2 While the soup is cooking, grill or fry the bacon until crisp, then cut it into strips. Shred the cabbage, discarding the core, and set aside.

3 Whizz the soup in the food processor until smooth then return it to the pan and add the cabbage. Simmer for a few minutes until the cabbage is just tender, then season to taste, drizzle with a little extra oil and serve scattered with the bacon strips.

PER SERVING 336 kcals, protein 21g, carbs 32g, fat 15g, sat fat 4g, fibre 5g, sugar 7g, salt 2.61g

Spicy prawn soup

Simply made in one pan, this Thai-style soup is packed with flavour. If you haven't got a can of coconut milk, use creamed coconut or a carton of coconut cream instead.

TAKES 20 MINUTES • SERVES 4

1 tbsp sunflower oil
300g bag crunchy stir-fry vegetables
140g/5oz shiitake mushrooms, sliced
2 tbsp Thai green curry paste
400ml can reduced-fat coconut milk
200ml/7fl oz vegetable or fish stock
300g/10oz straight-to-wok medium
   noodles
200g bag large raw peeled prawns

1 Heat the oil in a wok then add the sliced vegetables and the mushrooms and stir-fry for 2-3 minutes. Take out all the vegetables and set aside, then tip the curry paste into the pan and fry for 1 minute.

2 Pour in the coconut milk and stock. Bring to the boil, drop in the noodles and prawns, then reduce the heat, and simmer for 4 minutes until the prawns are cooked through. Pour the vegetables into the wok, stir through and serve.

PER SERVING 327 kcals, protein 16g, carbs 32g, fat 17g, sat fat 10g, fibre 4g, sugar 4g, salt 0.97g

White bean & pesto pot

Low in fat and packed with veggie goodness, serve this Italian-style meal-in-bowl with chunks of crusty bread. It takes just 20 minutes to make in the microwave.

TAKES 20 MINUTES ● SERVES 4

1 tbsp olive oil
1 onion, finely chopped
2 garlic cloves, chopped
200g/8oz courgettes, diced
3 tomatoes, chopped
2 tbsp fresh pesto
600ml/1 pint vegetable stock
410g can cannellini beans, drained
    and rinsed
100g/4oz mixed frozen vegetables
25g/1oz freshly grated Parmesan,
    to garnish
warm crusty bread, to serve

1 Put the oil, onion and garlic into the base of a large microwave-proof bowl, cover with a plate and microwave on High for 2 minutes. Stir, then add the courgettes and tomatoes, re-cover and cook for a further 2 minutes. Stir and cook for a further 2 minutes.

2 Stir 1 tablespoon of the pesto into the vegetable stock. Add to the bowl along with the beans, frozen vegetables and some seasoning. Stir well, cover and microwave on High for 4 minutes. Test the courgettes and, if necessary, cook for a further 1 minute until tender.

3 Stir well, re-cover and leave to stand for 3 minutes. Ladle into bowls and top with the remaining pesto. Sprinkle over the Parmesan and serve with warm, crusty bread.

PER SERVING 249 kcals, protein 13g, carbs 25g, fat 11g, sat fat 3g, fibre 8g, sugar none, salt 1.89g

Spiced carrot & lentil soup

To ring the changes with this soup, give it a Moroccan flavour by adding a few teaspoons of harissa paste instead of the chilli flakes and cumin.

TAKES 25 MINUTES • SERVES 4

2 tsp cumin seeds
pinch of dried chilli flakes
2 tbsp olive oil
600g/1lb 5oz carrots, washed and
    coarsely grated (no need to peel)
140g/5oz split red lentils
1 litre/1¾ pints hot vegetable stock
    (from a cube is fine)
125ml/4fl oz milk
natural yogurt and flat-leaf parsley
    leaves, to garnish
warmed naan breads, to serve

1 Heat a large saucepan and dry-fry the cumin seeds and chilli flakes for 1 minute or until they start to jump around the pan and release their aromas. Scoop out about half of the seeds with a spoon and set aside.

2 Add the oil, carrot, lentils, stock and milk to the pan and bring to the boil. Simmer for 15 minutes until the lentils have swollen and softened.

3 Whizz the soup with a stick blender or in a food processor until smooth (or leave it chunky, if you prefer). Season to taste and finish with a dollop of yogurt, a sprinkling of the reserved toasted spices and some flat-leaf parsley leaves. Serve with warmed naan breads.

PER SERVING 238 kcals, protein 11g, carbs 34g, fat 7g, sat fat 1g, fibre 5g, sugar none, salt 0.25g

Chicken, lentil & sweetcorn chowder

Lentils are a healthy addition to soups as they are a great source of essential amino acids and the minerals folate and iron, plus they are also high in fibre.

TAKES 35 MINUTES ● SERVES 4

4 spring onions, trimmed and thinly sliced
850ml/1½ pints chicken stock
250g/9oz potatoes, diced
300ml/½ pint skimmed milk
250g/9oz boneless skinless chicken breasts, cut into small pieces
140g/5oz frozen or canned sweetcorn
410g can Puy lentils or green lentils, drained and rinsed
snipped chives, to garnish

1 Put the spring onions in a large pan with 6 tablespoons of the stock and some seasoning. Cover and cook for 2–3 minutes until softened. Add the potatoes, the rest of the stock and the milk. Bring to the boil and simmer gently, partially covered, for 10 minutes or until the potatoes are just tender.

2 Ladle out about a quarter of the mixture into a blender and whizz until smooth. Stir back into the pan.

3 Add the chicken pieces, sweetcorn and lentils to the pan, and cook for 5–7 minutes more or until the chicken is cooked. Check the seasoning and serve in warm bowls, scattered with snipped chives.

PER SERVING 252 kcals, protein 31g, carbs 29g, fat 2g, sat fat 1g, fibre 6g, sugar 5g, salt 0.75g

Prawn chowder with mashed potato

This is fill-you-up food at its best, and who'd guess it's low in fat? Whizzing sweetcorn in the blender gives this soup a rich, luxurious texture and thickens it, too.

TAKES 35 MINUTES • SERVES 4

400g can sweetcorn, drained
500g/1lb 2oz floury potatoes, cubed
2 tbsp milk
1 tbsp sunflower oil
1 bunch spring onions, finely chopped
1 tbsp tomato purée
1 tsp paprika
600ml/1 pint vegetable stock
200g/8oz small cooked peeled prawns,
    defrosted if frozen
4 rashers streaky bacon

1 Tip the sweetcorn into a food processor and blend to a purée. Boil the potatoes in salted water until tender. Drain, mash with the milk and season to taste; keep the mash warm.

2 Meanwhile, heat the oil in a large pan, add most of the spring onions and fry for 2 minutes until softened. Add the sweetcorn, tomato purée, paprika and stock. Bring to the boil, simmer for 5 minutes, then stir in the prawns.

3 Grill the bacon until crisp. Divide the soup among four bowls and spoon the mash into the centre of each. Break up the bacon and scatter over with the remaining spring onions.

PER SERVING 338 kcals, protein 21g, carbs 47g, fat 9g, sat fat 2g, fibre 4g, sugar 12g, salt 2.43g

Wild mushroom, bacon & barley broth

Dried porcini mushrooms give this soup a rich flavour, which the barley and vegetables soak up. Try it with a sprinkling of cheese – it lifts a bowl of soup into a meal in itself.

TAKES 1 HOUR 35 MINUTES

• **SERVES 6**

200g pack bacon lardons or rashers bacon, cut into small pieces

2 onions, chopped

4 medium carrots, chopped

3 celery sticks, chopped

2 garlic cloves, crushed

1 sprig each rosemary and thyme

30g pack dried porcini or dried mixed wild mushrooms

1 glass white wine

1.5 litres/2¾ pints chicken stock

175g/6oz pearl barley, well rinsed

1 small head spring greens, shredded

Parmesan or any strong hard cheese, grated, to garnish

1 Sizzle the lardons or bacon in a large pan for 10 minutes until golden, stirring. Stir in the veg, garlic and herbs, cover, and cook gently for 10 minutes.

2 Meanwhile, put the mushrooms into a jug, then fill up the jug with boiling water to the 600ml/1 pint mark. Leave to soak for 10 minutes.

3 Lift out the mushrooms with a slotted spoon and roughly chop; reserve the liquid. Turn up the heat under the pan with the veg mix and add the mushrooms. Cook for 1 minute, then pour in the wine. Let it evaporate right down, then pour the reserved liquid from the mushroom jug into the pan (avoiding the last drops as they can be gritty) and add the stock and barley. Simmer the soup for around 40 minutes until the barley is tender.

4 Lift out the herbs, add the greens and simmer for 5 minutes. Season and serve with the cheese.

PER SERVING 290 kcals, protein 18g, carbs 35g, fat 9g, sat fat 3g, fibre 5g, sugar 9g, salt 1.75g

Spiced chicken & lentil soup

Two types of lentil are used here – red ones to break down and thicken the soup, and green ones to give it a hearty texture.

TAKES 45 MINUTES • SERVES 4

1 tsp each cumin and coriander seeds
1 tbsp sunflower oil
1 small onion, finely chopped
2 garlic cloves, finely chopped
14 curry leaves, freeze-dried or fresh
½ tsp ground turmeric
1.3 litres/2¼ pints chicken stock
100g/4oz green lentils
100g/4oz red lentils
227g can chopped tomatoes
100g/4oz cooked chicken, cut into
    small cubes
150g pot natural yogurt
good handful of chopped coriander
    leaves

1 Heat a small pan and dry-fry the cumin and coriander seeds for around 1–2 minutes until they start to brown. Grind them using a pestle and mortar.

2 Heat the oil in a pan and fry the onion for 3–4 minutes. Stir in the garlic and curry leaves, then fry for a minute or so. Stir in the ground cumin and coriander and the turmeric, then pour in the stock and bring to the boil. Add the green lentils, then simmer, uncovered, for 10 minutes. Stir in the red lentils and simmer for 15 minutes until the soup has thickened.

3 Tip in the tomatoes and chicken, then heat through. Stir in 1 tablespoon of the yogurt and half the coriander leaves, and check the seasoning. Mix the rest of the yogurt and coriander together in a small bowl and serve separately so each person can swirl a spoonful on top of their soup.

PER SERVING 346 kcals, protein 33g, carbs 36g, fat 8g, sat fat 2g, fibre 5g, sugar 8g, salt 0.91g

Hot & sour Thai noodle soup

A delicate oriental soup packed with mushrooms, mangetout, peas and baby corn cobs. Crisply fried rice noodles make a ruffled top-knot.

TAKES 50 MINUTES • SERVES 4

FOR THE CRISPY NOODLES
25g/1oz thread rice noodles
oil, for shallow frying

FOR THE SOUP
2 lemongrass stalks, bruised
8cm/3in piece ginger, peeled and sliced
2 red bird's-eye chillies, halved and deseeded
handful of coriander leaves, chopped
4 kaffir lime leaves, bruised
2 plum tomatoes, chopped
1 tbsp chilli or vegetable oil
200g/8oz small shiitake mushrooms, halved
2 tbsp dark soy sauce
100g/4oz mangetout, trimmed and shredded
140g/5oz baby corn cobs, halved lengthways
100g/4oz frozen peas

1 Soak the noodles according to the packet instructions. Rinse, drain and pat dry. Put the lemongrass, ginger, chillies, coriander, lime leaves and tomatoes in a large pan with 1.5 litres/2¾ pints water, bring to the boil and simmer for around 15 minutes. Strain and reserve.

2 Heat the oil in a large pan and stir-fry the mushrooms for 1–2 minutes. Add the infused stock, soy sauce, mangetout, corn cobs and peas. Bring to the boil and simmer for 2 minutes. Keep warm.

3 Pour oil into a wok to a depth of 2cm/¾in and heat until a piece of bread turns golden in 30 seconds. Add a few of the noodles and cook for 10 seconds until puffed up and crisp. Lift out and drain on kitchen paper. Cook the remaining noodles in the same way. Divide the soup among bowls and pile the crispy noodles on top to serve.

PER SERVING 108 kcals, protein 5g, carbs 12g, fat 5g, sat fat 1g, fibre 3g, sugar none, salt 1.18g

Raviolini & rosemary consommé

This clear soup is made special by adding some cheese-filled ravioli – it looks pretty and tastes good. Add to the Italian flavours by sprinkling it with Parmesan.

TAKES 1 HOUR 20 MINUTES
- **SERVES 4**

1 onion, roughly chopped
3 carrots, roughly chopped
1 leek, roughly chopped
3 celery sticks, sliced
4 large rosemary sprigs, bruised
1 bay leaf
250g pack cheese-filled raviolini (mini ravioli)
6 plum tomatoes, skinned, deseeded and roughly chopped
handful of basil leaves, torn, to garnish

1 Put the onion, carrots, leek, celery, rosemary, bay leaf and 1.7 litres/3 pints water in a large pan. Bring to the boil, cover, and simmer for 1 hour.

2 Skim off any scum, then pour through a sieve into a clean pan (don't press the vegetables as this will make the stock cloudy). Stir a few of the tender rosemary leaves back into the pan.

3 Bring back to the boil, add the raviolini and simmer for 3 minutes. Stir in the tomatoes and cook for 2 minutes to warm through. Season to taste. Divide the soup among serving bowls and scatter with torn basil leaves.

PER SERVING 153 kcals, protein 6g, carbs 21g, fat 5g, sat fat 3g, fibre 4g, sugar none, salt 0.3g

Chunky minestrone

Here's a warming classic of veggie goodness that provides your 5-a-day in one bowl.
Good flavour and texture combine in this comforting, low-fat meal.

TAKES 45 MINUTES • SERVES 4

3 large carrots, roughly chopped
1 large onion, roughly chopped
4 celery sticks, roughly chopped
1 tbsp olive oil
2 garlic cloves, crushed
2 large potatoes, cut into small dice
2 tbsp tomato purée
2 litres/3½ pints vegetable stock
400g can chopped tomatoes
400g can cannellini or butter beans,
  drained and rinsed
140g/5oz spaghetti, snapped into short
  lengths
½ head Savoy cabbage, shredded
crusty bread, to serve

1 In a food processor, whizz the carrots, onion and celery into small pieces. Heat the oil in a pan, add the processed vegetables, garlic and potatoes, then cook the mixture over a high heat for 5 minutes until softened.

2 Stir in the tomato purée, stock and tomatoes. Bring to the boil, then turn down the heat and simmer, covered, for 10 minutes.

3 Tip in the beans and pasta, then cook for a further 10 minutes, adding the cabbage for the final 2 minutes. Season to taste and serve with crusty bread.

PER SERVING 420 kcals, protein 18g, carbs 79g, fat 6g, sat fat 1g, fibre 16g, sugar 24g, salt 1.11g

Chicken noodle soup

Soothing and comforting, this aromatic broth is packed with favourite flavours and makes a satisfying bowlful that looks good, tastes good and makes you feel good.

TAKES 40 MINUTES • SERVES 2

850ml/1½ pints chicken or vegetable stock
1 boneless skinless chicken breast, about 175g/6oz
1 tsp chopped ginger
1 garlic clove, finely chopped
50g/2oz rice or wheat noodles
2 tbsp sweetcorn, canned or frozen
2–3 mushrooms, thinly sliced
2 spring onions, shredded
2 tsp soy sauce, plus extra to taste
mint or basil leaves and a little shredded chilli (optional), to garnish

1 Pour the stock into a pan and add the chicken, ginger and garlic. Bring to the boil, then reduce the heat, partly cover, and simmer for 20 minutes until the chicken is tender. Remove the chicken to a board and shred into bite-sized pieces using a couple of forks.

2 Return the chicken to the stock with the noodles, sweetcorn, mushrooms, half the spring onions and the soy sauce. Simmer for 3–4 minutes until the noodles are tender. Ladle into two bowls and scatter over the remaining spring onions, and the herbs and chilli shreds, if using. Serve with extra soy sauce sprinkled over the soup.

PER SERVING 217 kcals, protein 26g, carbs 26g, fat 2g, sat fat 0.4g, fibre 0.6g, sugar 1g, salt 2.52g

Easy noodle soup

A real winner with the kids and ready in under 25 minutes, this is the perfect lunchtime meal. It's also satisfying and low in fat.

TAKES 23 MINUTES ● SERVES 2

500ml/18fl oz low-salt vegetable stock (from a cube is fine)
small piece of ginger, grated
1 garlic clove, grated
2 tsp soy sauce
2 tsp sugar
85g/3oz cooked chicken, shredded
handful of mixed vegetables (try beansprouts, sweetcorn, sliced carrot and mangetout)
150g pack straight-to-wok noodles (or use 85g/3oz dried noodles, cooked according to the packet instructions)
2 spring onions, sliced, to garnish
juice of 1 lime, to taste

1 Heat the stock, ginger, garlic, soy sauce and sugar in a pan. Simmer for 5 minutes then take the pan off the heat and pour the mixture into a microwave-proof bowl.

2 Throw in the chicken and veg, then add the noodles. Microwave on High for 2 minutes, stir, then cook for 1 minute more or until piping hot. Divide between two bowls or mugs, sprinkle with the sliced spring onions and add the lime juice to taste.

PER SERVING 241 kcals, protein 18g, carbs 36g, fat 4g, sat fat 1g, fibre 2g, sugar 7g, salt 2.03g

Pea & bacon chowder

Cosy up on the sofa on a cold night with a warming bowl or mug of this slimline chowder – easy to make and even easier to eat.

TAKES 35 MINUTES • SERVES 4

1 tbsp olive oil
1 onion, finely chopped
1 garlic clove, crushed
650g/1lb 7oz frozen petits pois
850ml/1½ pints vegetable stock
6 rashers streaky bacon
1 tbsp butter (optional)

1 Heat the oil in a pan, add the onion and gently cook over a medium heat for 5–6 minutes until softened but not coloured. Add the garlic and cook for a further minute. Stir in three-quarters of the petits pois then pour in the stock. Bring the soup to the boil and simmer for 10–12 minutes.

2 Meanwhile, grill the bacon until crisp. Allow the soup to cool for a few minutes, then transfer to a food processor and whizz until smooth.

3 Return the soup to the pan and add the remaining petits pois. Bring to the boil and simmer for 2 minutes or until the whole peas are tender. Season to taste, then stir in the butter, if using. Break the bacon into pieces and scatter over bowls or mugs of soup.

PER SERVING 131 kcals, protein 11g, carbs 12g, fat 5g, sat fat 1g, fibre 6g, sugar 4g, salt 1.11g

Haddock & sweetcorn soup

Satisfying and packed with veg, this slender soup makes a complete meal when served with crispy mini pittas topped with soft cheese, mustard and ham.

TAKES 30 MINUTES ● SERVES 4

3 medium potatoes, peeled
  and chopped
600ml/1 pint full-fat milk
500ml/18fl oz hot fish stock
400g/14oz skinless smoked haddock
  fillet, cut into large chunks
200g/8oz broccoli, chopped
2 × 198g cans sweetcorn, drained
squeeze of fresh lemon juice
2 spring onions, thinly sliced, to garnish

1 Put the potatoes into a large pan with the milk and fish stock. Bring to the boil, then simmer for about 10 minutes until tender. Mash some of the potatoes into the liquid with a potato masher.

2 Stir in the haddock and broccoli, then simmer for 5 minutes until the fish is flaky and the broccoli is just tender. Stir in the sweetcorn and lemon juice, then warm through. Scatter over the spring onions to serve.

PER SERVING 360 kcals, protein 31g, carbs 43g, fat 8g, sat fat 4g, fibre 4g, sugar 16g, salt 3.63g

Hearty ham & cabbage broth

Wholesome and tasty, this really does make a meal in a bowl with the vegetables, ham and pasta. A chunk of crusty bread is the only accompaniment you'll need.

TAKES 20 MINUTES ● SERVES 4

1 tbsp olive oil
2 onions, finely chopped
1 carrot, finely chopped
2 large potatoes, cut into small cubes
50g/2oz ham off the bone, shredded
1.2 litres/2 pints hot vegetable stock
　(from a cube is fine)
50g/2oz small pasta shapes or broken
　spaghetti
½ Savoy cabbage, shredded
crusty bread, to serve

1 Heat the oil in a large pan and tip in the chopped onions and carrot. Fry gently for 5 minutes until softened, but not coloured. Add the potatoes, ham and stock, bring to the boil, then simmer for 10 minutes until the potato is almost cooked. Tip in the pasta and cook for a further 8–10 minutes until the pasta is tender and the potatoes have started to break down and thicken the soup.
2 Stir the cabbage through the soup and simmer for another 1–2 minutes until just cooked. Season to taste with black pepper and serve with crusty bread.

PER SERVING 219 kcals, protein 10g, carbs 37g, fat 4g, sat fat 1g, fibre 6g, sugar 1g, salt 1.42g

15-minute summer soup

The watercress and mint just need to be barely wilted in this recipe to retain the most wonderful peppery flavour and fresh colour.

TAKES 15 MINUTES • SERVES 4

knob of butter or splash of olive oil
1 bunch spring onions, chopped
3 courgettes, chopped
200g/8oz podded fresh or frozen peas
850ml/1½ pints hot vegetable stock
85g bag trimmed watercress
large handful of mint leaves
2 rounded tbsp 0% fat Greek yogurt, plus extra for drizzling

1 Heat the butter or oil in a pan, add the spring onions and courgettes, and stir well. Cover and cook for 3 minutes, add the peas and stock, and return to the boil. Cover and simmer for a further 4 minutes, then remove from the heat and stir in the watercress and mint until they are wilted.

2 Purée in a food processor, adding the yogurt with the second batch. Return to the pan, then add seasoning to taste. Serve the soup hot or cold, drizzled with extra yogurt.

PER SERVING 100 kcals, protein 8g, carbs 9g, fat 4g, sat fat 2g, fibre 4g, sugar none, salt 0.81g

Chicken & watercress soup

Need a superquick but healthy lunch? Try this hassle-free light soup that's made in just 10 minutes and is packed with goodness.

TAKES 10 MINUTES • SERVES 4

1.2 litres/2 pints chicken stock (from a cube is fine)
100g pack shiitake mushrooms, thickly sliced
2 cooked boneless skinless chicken breasts, shredded
100g bag watercress
2 tsp sesame oil

1 Pour the stock into a large pan and bring to a simmer. Add the mushrooms and cook for 5 minutes.

2 Stir in the chicken and watercress, turn off the heat and season with the sesame oil and a sprinkling of salt, if needed. Give the soup several stirs and allow to sit for 2 minutes before serving.

PER SERVING 125 kcals, protein 21g, carbs 1g, fat 4g, sat fat 1g, fibre 0.4g, sugar 0.1g, salt 1.16g

Hearty mushroom soup

Porcini mushrooms are wild mushrooms that have been dried. They are great as a substitute for fresh mushrooms, or they can be used to boost their flavour.

TAKES 1 HOUR ● SERVES 4–6

25g pack porcini mushrooms
2 tbsp olive oil
1 medium onion, finely diced
2 large carrots, diced
2 garlic cloves, finely chopped
1 tbsp chopped rosemary or 1 tsp dried
500g/1lb 2oz mushrooms, such as chestnut, finely chopped
1.2 litres/2 pints vegetable stock (from a cube is fine)
5 tbsp Marsala or dry sherry
2 tbsp tomato purée
100g/4oz pearl barley
grated Parmesan, to sprinkle (optional)

1 Put the porcini in a bowl with 225ml/8fl oz boiling water and leave to soak for 25 minutes. Heat the oil in a pan and add the onion, carrot, garlic, rosemary and seasoning. Fry for 5 minutes on a medium heat until the mixture has softened.

2 Drain the porcini, saving the liquid, and finely chop. Tip into the pan with the fresh mushrooms. Fry for another 5 minutes, then add the stock, Marsala or sherry, tomato purée, barley and strained porcini liquid. Cook for around 30 minutes or until the barley is soft, adding more liquid if it becomes too thick. Serve in bowls with Parmesan sprinkled over, if desired.

PER SERVING 245 kcals, protein 8g, carbs 35g, fat 7g, sat fat 1g, fibre 3g, sugar 10g, salt 1.13g

Salsa soup

This light, tomato-flavoured soup doesn't even need cooking, and it's healthy, too – it provides two of your 5-a-day and is full of vitamin C.

TAKES 10 MINUTES ● SERVES 2

5 ripe tomatoes, about 300g/10oz,
   chopped into large chunks
1 small red onion, chopped
1 garlic clove, chopped
½ tsp sugar
juice of 1 lime
handful of coriander, stalks and leaves
   chopped
olive oil, to drizzle
tortilla chips, to serve

1 Tip the first six ingredients into a blender or food processor, reserving a little coriander, and season with a generous grinding of salt and black pepper, if you like. Pulse until you get a chunky, frothy soup.

2 Serve the soup straight away, drizzled with a little olive oil and with the tortilla chips on the side, or chill until needed.

PER SERVING 74 kcals, protein 2g, carbs 9g, fat 4g, sat fat 1g, fibre 2g, sugar 8g, salt 0.42g

Red lentil, chickpea & chilli soup

This healthy, warming soup contains three of your 5-a-day. Cans of tomatoes range in price – look out for good-value Italian brands as they often have a better flavour.

TAKES 35 MINUTES • SERVES 4

2 tsp cumin seeds
large pinch of chilli flakes
1 tbsp olive oil
1 red onion, chopped
140g/5oz red split lentils
850ml/1½ pints vegetable stock or
    water
400g can tomatoes, whole or chopped
200g carton chickpeas or ½ × 400g
    can, drained and rinsed (freeze
    the leftovers)
small bunch of coriander, roughly
    chopped (save a few leaves to
    garnish)
4 tbsp 0% fat Greek yogurt, to garnish

1 Heat a large pan and dry-fry the cumin seeds and chilli flakes for 1 minute or until they start to jump around the pan and release their aromas. Add the oil and onion, and cook for 5 minutes. Stir in the lentils, stock or water and tomatoes, then bring to the boil. Simmer the soup for 15 minutes until the lentils have softened.

2 Whizz the soup with an electric stick blender or in a food processor until it is a rough purée, pour back into the pan and add the chickpeas. Heat gently, season well and stir in the coriander. Serve in warm bowls topped with a dollop of yogurt and the reserved coriander.

PER SERVING 222 kcals, protein 13g, carbs 33g, fat 5g, sat fat none, fibre 6g, sugar 6g, salt 0.87g

Polish sausage soup

Kabanos are firm, meaty smoked sausages from Poland and are widely available from supermarkets. You could also use Spanish chorizo for this substantial soup.

TAKES 40 MINUTES • SERVES 4

2 large onions, sliced
2 tbsp olive oil
2 garlic cloves, thinly sliced
200g/8oz kabanos sausages, chopped
1 tsp paprika, sweet or smoked
85g/3oz brown basmati rice
1 tbsp chopped thyme leaves
2 litres/3½ pints strong-flavoured
    beef stock
3 carrots, thickly sliced
100g/4oz shredded kale
crusty bread, to serve

1 Fry the onions in the oil for 5 minutes. Add the garlic and sausage, fry for a few minutes more, then stir in the paprika, rice and thyme.

2 Pour in the stock and bring to the boil. Add the carrots and some salt and pepper, cover, then simmer the soup for 20 minutes. Stir in the shredded kale, then cook for a further 10 minutes. Serve with chunks of crusty bread.

PER SERVING 433 kcals, protein 21g, carbs 34g, fat 24g, sat fat 6g, fibre 5g, sugar 12g, salt 3.83g

Kale & chorizo broth

If you prefer a smoother finish, fish out the chorizo after step 1, blend the potato base, then return the chorizo to the pan when you add the kale.

TAKES 45 MINUTES • SERVES 6
3 tbsp olive oil
2 onions, finely chopped
4 garlic cloves, crushed
2–3 cooking chorizo sausages, sliced
4 large potatoes, chopped
1.5 litres/2¾ pints chicken stock
200g/8oz kale, finely shredded

1 Heat 2 tablespoons of the oil in a large pan. Add the onions, garlic and chorizo, then cook for 5 minutes until soft. Throw in the potatoes and cook for a few minutes more. Pour in the stock, season, and bring to the boil. Cook everything for 10 minutes until the potatoes are on the brink of collapse.

2 Use a masher to squash the potatoes into the soup, then bring back to the boil. Add the kale and cook for 5 minutes until tender. Ladle the soup into bowls, then serve drizzled with the remaining olive oil.

PER SERVING 314 kcals, protein 19g, carbs 30g, fat 14g, sat fat 3g, fibre 4g, sugar 5g, salt 1.7g

Leek, bacon & potato soup

Bacon is a tasty addition to this classic combo. This soup will keep in the fridge for a couple of days, but if you want to freeze it, don't add the cream until you reheat it.

TAKES 1 HOUR • SERVES 4–6

25g/1oz butter

3 rashers streaky bacon, chopped, plus 4 extra rashers, fried until crisp, to garnish

1 onion, chopped

400g pack trimmed leeks, sliced and well washed

3 medium potatoes, peeled and diced

1.4 litres/2½ pints hot vegetable stock

142ml pot single cream

toasted or warm crusty bread, to serve

1 Melt the butter in a large pan then fry the bacon and onion, stirring until they start to turn golden. Tip in the leeks and potatoes, stir well, then cover and turn down the heat. Cook gently for around 5 minutes, shaking the pan every now and then to make sure that the mixture doesn't catch.

2 Pour in the stock, season well and bring to the boil. Cover and simmer for 20 minutes until the vegetables are soft. Leave to cool for a few minutes, then blend in a food processor in batches until smooth.

3 Return to the pan, pour in the cream and stir well. Taste and season, if necessary. Serve scattered with tasty, crisp bacon and eat with toasted or warm, crusty bread on the side.

PER SERVING (6) 175 kcals, protein 6g, carbs 15g, fat 11g, sat fat 6g, fibre 4g, sugar 5g, salt 0.68g

Cream of wild mushroom soup

This rich and filling dish is the perfect way to use up end-of-season mushrooms on the cheap. Just right for a family lunch or special enough for entertaining friends.

TAKES 1 HOUR 10 MINUTES

● **SERVES 4**

25g/1oz dried porcini mushrooms (ceps)

50g/2oz butter

1 onion, finely chopped

1 garlic clove, sliced

a few thyme sprigs

400g/14oz mixed wild mushrooms

850ml/1½ pints vegetable stock

200ml pot crème fraîche

4 slices white bread, about 100g/4oz, cubed

snipped chives and truffle oil, to garnish

1 Pour some boiling water over the dried porcini, just to cover. Heat half the butter in a pan, then gently sizzle the onion, garlic and thyme for 5 minutes until softened and starting to brown.

2 Drain the porcini, reserving and straining the soaking liquid, then add to the onion with the mixed wild mushrooms. Leave to cook for 5 minutes until they go limp. Pour over the stock and the reserved porcini juices, bring to the boil, then simmer for 20 minutes.

3 Stir in the crème fraîche, then simmer for a few minutes more. Blitz the soup with an electric hand blender or liquidiser and pass through a fine sieve.

4 Heat the remaining butter in a frying pan, fry the bread cubes until golden, then drain on kitchen paper. Heat the soup and ladle into bowls, scatter over the croutons and chives, and drizzle with truffle oil.

PER SERVING 347 kcals, protein 8g, carbs 20g, fat 27g, sat fat 16g, fibre 4g, sugar 5g, salt 0.89g

Spiced carrot soup with Asian salad

A rich, aromatic soup topped with a crisp Asian-salad garnish that adds texture. If you can't find curry leaves, add 1 teaspoon of curry paste to the stir-fried salad mixture.

TAKES 50 MINUTES ● SERVES 4

1 large onion, finely chopped

2 tsp crushed garlic

2 tsp finely chopped ginger

1 tbsp medium–hot curry paste

420g can yellow split peas, drained and rinsed

450g/1lb carrots, coarsely grated

1.2 litres/2 pints vegetable stock

2 tbsp vegetable oil

24 fresh curry leaves

2 tsp onion seeds

300g bag vegetable stir-fry mix

1 Dry-fry the onion and half the garlic and ginger for 2 minutes in a large non-stick pan – add a splash of water if they start to catch. Stir in the curry paste and cook for 1 minute. Stir in the split peas, carrots and stock, bring to the boil and simmer for 25 minutes. Transfer the split-pea mixture to a food processor or blender and process until smooth. Return to the pan, heat through and season to taste.

2 Heat the oil in a wok or large frying pan and fry the curry leaves and onion seeds over a high heat for 1 minute until the seeds start to pop. Add the remaining garlic and ginger and the vegetable stir-fry mix, and stir-fry for 2 minutes.

3 Divide the soup among serving bowls and pile a little of the stir-fried salad on top of each. Serve immediately.

PER SERVING 311 kcals, protein 15g, carbs 42g, fat 10g, sat fat 1g, fibre 6g, sugar none, salt 1.4g

Tom Yam noodle soup

There are many versions of this traditional Thai soup and this is a vegetarian one. You should check the curry paste you use is suitable for vegetarians.

TAKES 35 MINUTES • SERVES 2

1 tbsp sunflower oil

2 shallots, finely chopped

2 crushed garlic cloves

140g/5oz button mushrooms, sliced

1 red pepper, deseeded and cut into small strips

2 tsp Thai red curry paste

850ml/1½ pints vegetable stock

1 tbsp soy sauce

finely grated zest of 1 lime and juice of ½

100g/4oz egg noodles

220g can bamboo shoots, drained and rinsed

15g pack coriander, leaves roughly torn

1 Heat the oil in a pan and fry the shallots for 4–5 minutes until golden. Stir in the garlic, mushrooms and red pepper, and fry for 3 minutes.

2 Add the curry paste and cook for 1 minute. Stir in the stock, soy sauce and lime zest. Simmer for 3–4 minutes then add the noodles and simmer for 4 minutes until the noodles are cooked.

3 Add the bamboo shoots and around two-thirds of the coriander and cook for 2 minutes. Twist the noodles into nests using a large fork and spoon, and put in individual soup bowls. Add the lime juice to the soup, to taste. Pour the soup around the noodles and garnish with the remaining coriander.

PER SERVING 393 kcals, protein 15g, carbs 55g, fat 14g, sat fat 1g, fibre 7g, sugar none, salt 2.77g

Sweetcorn & smoky pepper chowder

A warming and delicious way to use up frozen sweetcorn – often a permanent and stubborn feature in your freezer! If you don't like your food too spicy, only use one chilli.

TAKES 40 MINUTES • SERVES 4

2 large red chillies
3 red peppers
2 tbsp olive oil
1 small onion, finely chopped
2 garlic cloves, crushed
1.5 litres/2¾ pints vegetable stock
800g/1lb 12oz potatoes, cut into 2cm/¾in cubes
450g/1lb frozen sweetcorn kernels, thawed
6 spring onions, finely sliced
6 tbsp chopped coriander leaves
150ml/¼ pint double cream
warm pitta bread, to serve

1 Heat the grill to high. Grill the chillies and peppers for 5–10 minutes, turning frequently, until the skin is lightly charred. Put them in a plastic bag and leave to cool. Peel off the skins, deseed and roughly chop the flesh.

2 Heat the oil in a large pan. Add the onion and cook for 5 minutes until softened. Add the garlic and cook for a further 2 minutes. Add the vegetable stock and potatoes, bring to the boil and simmer for 10 minutes until tender.

3 Allow to cool slightly. Process to a coarse purée in a food processor (you may need to do this in batches). Return the mixture to the pan and bring to the boil. Add the sweetcorn, chilli, peppers and spring onions, and simmer for 2 minutes. Stir in the chopped coriander and cream. Season and serve the soup with warm pitta bread.

PER SERVING 565 kcals, protein 13g, carbs 68g, fat 29g, sat fat 13g, fibre 7g, sugar none, salt 1.35g

Spicy kidney bean soup

Here the hot notes of chilli and spices are perfectly partnered with a cool mayonnaise topping to make a substantial, satisfying soup.

TAKES 1 HOUR • SERVES 4

1 large onion, roughly chopped
4 garlic cloves, finely chopped
3 celery sticks, sliced
3–4 red bird's-eye chillies, deseeded
    and finely chopped
2 carrots, finely diced
2 tbsp olive oil
2 tsp each ground coriander, cumin
    and mild chilli powder
250ml/9fl oz red wine
420g can red kidney beans, drained
    and rinsed
1.7 litres/3 pints vegetable stock
1 red and 1 yellow pepper
finely grated zest and juice of 2 limes
3 tbsp chopped flat-leaf parsley, plus
    sprigs to garnish
mayonnaise and sweet chilli sauce,
    to garnish

1 Fry the onion, garlic, celery, chillies and carrots in the oil for 12–15 minutes, stirring occasionally. Stir in the spices and cook for 1–2 minutes. Add the wine and boil rapidly for 3 minutes. Stir in the beans and stock, and bring to the boil. Reduce the heat, cover, and simmer gently for 10 minutes.

2 Deseed and finely chop the peppers. Transfer half the bean mixture to a food processor and process until almost smooth. Stir back into the remaining bean mixture along with the peppers, lime zest and juice and parsley. Bring to the boil, then simmer for 5 minutes, stirring. Season to taste.

3 Divide the soup among four bowls and top with some mayonnaise and sweet chilli sauce. Garnish with sprigs of flat-leaf parsley.

PER SERVING 407 kcals, protein 13g, carbs 33g, fat 21g, sat fat 3g, fibre 9g, sugar none, salt 2.69g

Moroccan vegetable soup with couscous

A fusion of the colours of the souk, this contemporary mixture is complemented by the calm neutral of the couscous. Harissa is a widely available Moroccan chilli paste.

TAKES 55 MINUTES • SERVES 4

100g/4oz couscous
4 tbsp olive oil
1 small aubergine, cut into 2cm/¾in chunks
2 large onions, roughly chopped
2 garlic cloves, crushed
1 large baking potato, cut into 2cm/¾in chunks
2 large carrots, thickly sliced
400g can chopped tomatoes
2 tbsp tomato purée
1 litre/1¾ pints vegetable stock
2 courgettes, cut into 2cm/¾in chunks
3–4 tsp harissa paste
2 tbsp chopped mint leaves, plus sprigs to garnish
2 tbsp chopped coriander leaves

1 Spread the couscous over the bottom of a shallow dish, pour over 200ml/7fl oz boiling water and leave to soak for 20 minutes.

2 Meanwhile, heat the oil in a large pan and fry the aubergine for 5–6 minutes, stirring occasionally, until it is lightly browned. Stir in the onions, garlic, potato and carrots, and cook for 3 minutes. Add the tomatoes, tomato purée and stock. Bring to the boil and simmer for 15–20 minutes until almost tender, stirring occasionally. Stir in the courgettes and harissa, and cook for a further 5 minutes, stirring frequently.

3 Fluff up the couscous with a fork and season to taste. Stir through the mint and coriander. Divide the soup among individual serving bowls and just before serving pile the couscous in the centre. Garnish with the sprigs of mint.

PER SERVING 327 kcals, protein 8g, carbs 40g, fat 16g, sat fat 2g, fibre 5g, sugar none, salt 1.04g.

Tuscan bean soup

This combination is inspired by the colours and flavours of the Italian countryside. Ebly is whole, pre-cooked durum wheat grains and is available from most supermarkets.

TAKES 45 MINUTES • SERVES 6

FOR THE SOUP

200g/8oz Ebly

2 tbsp extra-virgin olive oil

2 rosemary sprigs, leaves only

3 garlic cloves, crushed

150ml/¼ pint dry white wine

2 x 420g cans mixed pulses, drained and rinsed

420g can chickpeas, drained and rinsed

400g can chopped tomatoes with herbs

300ml/½ pint vegetable stock

175g/6oz Savoy cabbage, shredded

FOR THE CROUTES

3 tbsp extra-virgin olive oil

2 tbsp thyme leaves

2 garlic cloves, quartered

6 thin diagonal slices baguette

1 Bring a large pan of water to the boil, add the Ebly and cook for 15 minutes. Rinse in cold water and drain well. Heat the oil in a large pan and fry the rosemary and garlic for 2 minutes. Stir in the wine and simmer for around 2 minutes. Stir in half the drained pulses and chickpeas and all the tomatoes, and bring to the boil.

2 Process in a food processor until smooth. Return to the pan and add the reserved pulses and chickpeas, stock and wheat grains. Cook gently for 6–8 minutes, stirring, until piping hot.

3 For the croûtes, gently heat the oil, thyme and garlic in a pan for 2 minutes. Brush both sides of the bread with the oil. Heat a dry griddle pan until hot and toast the bread quickly.

4 Boil the cabbage in a pan of water for 1 minute, then drain. Spoon the soup into warmed bowls and top with the cooked cabbage and croûtes.

PER SERVING 502 kcals, protein 20g, carbs 68g, fat 17g, sat fat 2g, fibre 13g, sugar 0.1g, salt 2.32g

Leek, barley & chickpea soup

This wintry soup tastes even better when left overnight, allowing the flavours to really develop. It makes an ideal hearty supper for entertaining family or friends.

TAKES 1 HOUR 25 MINUTES
- **SERVES 8**

3 leeks, sliced into 2cm/¾in rings
2 Spanish onions, roughly chopped
1 large carrot, roughly chopped
2 celery sticks, roughly chopped
5 tbsp olive oil
1 orange
2 garlic cloves, crushed
1 red chilli, deseeded and finely
　chopped
1 tsp caster sugar
2 tomatoes, roughly chopped
400g can chickpeas, rinsed and drained
2.5 litres/4½ pints vegetable stock (a
　cube is fine)
1 rosemary sprig
1 bay leaf
250g/9oz pearl barley
grated cheese, to garnish
crusty bread, to serve

1 Tip the leeks, onions, carrot, celery and olive oil into a large pan. Cook over a low heat for 5 minutes, stirring often, until the vegetables start to soften. Finely grate the zest of the orange and add to the pan with the garlic, chilli and sugar. Cook for 1 minute longer, then add the tomatoes and squeeze over the juice of the orange.

2 Tip in the chickpeas, vegetable stock, rosemary and bay leaf. Bring to the boil, then leave to simmer for 20 minutes. Add the barley and simmer for another 40 minutes until the barley is cooked. Season with salt and black pepper. Sprinkle with grated cheese and serve with some crusty bread.

PER SERVING 267 kcals, protein 8g, carbs 41g, fat 9g, sat fat 1g, fibre 4g, sugar 1g, salt 1.24g

Spring greens & gammon soup

This rustic broth is deliciously meaty and worth cooking a gammon for, or you can use up leftover ham. Healthy and hearty, it's low in fat too.

TAKES 2 HOURS 10 MINUTES

● **SERVES 4**

450g/1lb piece gammon, soaked
   overnight

2 bay leaves

2 medium onions, sliced

2 tsp paprika

2 large potatoes, peeled and chopped
   into small chunks

200g/8oz spring greens, finely
   shredded

400g can cannellini beans, drained
   and rinsed

1 Put the gammon in a large pan with the bay leaves, onions and about 1.5 litres/2¾ pints cold water, or enough to cover. Bring to the boil, then reduce the heat and simmer gently for about 1½ hours. Drain the gammon, reserving the cooking liquid. When the gammon is cool enough to handle, trim away the skin and shred the meat.

2 Return the meat to the pan with the reserved cooking liquid, paprika and potatoes. Cover and simmer the soup for 20 minutes or until the potatoes are cooked.

3 Stir the greens and beans into the soup, and continue to cook for about 10 minutes until cooked. Season to taste and serve.

PER SERVING 350 kcals, protein 30g, carbs 32g, fat 12g, sat fat 4g, fibre 7g, sugar 4g, salt 3.33g

Cauliflower cheese soup

Soup and cauliflower cheese are both real comfort foods and this dish is a perfect combination of the two. Great for handing round at Halloween or on Bonfire Night.

TAKES 45 MINUTES • SERVES 6

knob of butter
1 large onion, finely chopped
1 large cauliflower (about 900g/2lb), leaves trimmed and cut into florets
1 potato, peeled and cut into chunks
700ml/1¼ pints vegetable stock (from a cube is fine)
400ml/14fl oz milk, plus extra to thin (optional)
100g/4oz mature Cheddar, diced

1 Heat the butter in a large pan then tip in the onion and cook for about 5 minutes until softened, stirring often. Add the cauliflower, potato, stock, milk and seasoning. Bring to the boil, then reduce the heat and leave to simmer for about 30 minutes until the cauliflower is soft and the potato almost collapsing.

2 Whizz in a food processor or crush with a potato masher until you get a creamy, thick soup. (Top up with more milk to thin the soup a little if you are serving it in mugs.) Warm through, ladle into mugs or bowls, top with the cheese dices and stir through before eating.

PER SERVING 188 kcals, protein 13g, carbs 13g, fat 10g, sat fat 5g, fibre 3g, sugar 9g, salt 0.82g

Mushroom & chestnut soup

Make the most of fresh mushrooms when they're in season in the autumn.
Their earthy flavour works well with chestnuts for this winter warmer.

TAKES 40 MINUTES • SERVES 4

2 tbsp olive oil
1 onion, chopped
1 garlic clove, crushed
375g/13oz mixed mushrooms
  (chestnut, shiitake, oyster and
  field), sliced
15g pack thyme, leaves chopped,
  reserving 4 sprigs to garnish
435g can chestnut purée
1 litre/1¾ pints vegetable stock
2 tbsp sherry (optional)
4 tbsp soured cream

1 Heat the oil in a pan and fry the onion for 2–3 minutes until softened. Add the garlic and fry for a further 1–2 minutes. Stir in the sliced mushrooms and fry for 3–4 minutes, stirring occasionally, until golden. Remove half the mushrooms and set aside.

2 Add the chopped thyme, chestnut purée and stock to the mushroom mixture in the pan. Bring to the boil, cover, and simmer for 10–15 minutes. Remove from the heat and blend with an electric hand blender or in a food processor until smooth.

3 Add all but 4 tablespoons of the reserved mushrooms and sherry, if using, to the soup and stir over a low heat until piping hot. Season to taste. Spoon into serving bowls and top with the remaining fried mushrooms, the soured cream and whole thyme sprigs. Sprinkle with black pepper and serve.

PER SERVING 323 kcals, protein 6g, carbs 44g, fat 14g, sat fat 4g, fibre 6g, sugar 0.1g, salt 0.91g

Spicy pasta soup

This budget-beating soup is easily made from storecupboard ingredients. Packed with goodness, it's a good source of vitamin C and counts as two of your 5-a-day.

TAKES 45 MINUTES • SERVES 4

1 tbsp olive oil, plus extra for drizzling
1 red onion, finely chopped
1 red chilli, deseeded and finely sliced
800g can whole plum tomatoes
1 litre/1¾ pints vegetable stock
100g/4oz broken spaghetti
4 tbsp chopped pitted black olives
2 tbsp chopped capers, drained and rinsed
large handful of basil leaves, roughly torn, or 1 tbsp pesto

1 Heat the oil in a large heavy-based pan. Add the onion and chilli, then cook for 10 minutes until softened. Stir in the tomatoes, breaking them up with a spoon as you go, then pour in the stock. Cover, bring to the boil, remove the lid, then simmer for 5 minutes.

2 Add the spaghetti, then simmer for 6–8 minutes until it is just cooked. Stir in the olives, capers and the basil or pesto, then serve drizzled with olive oil.

PER SERVING 218 kcals, protein 7g, carbs 29g, fat 9g, sat fat 1g, fibre 5g, sugar 10g, salt 1.20g

Spiced citrus bean soup

The beans give a nice texture to this soup and the coconut milk adds a delicious creaminess. Naan bread makes the ideal accompaniment.

TAKES 50 MINUTES • SERVES 4

2 tbsp olive oil
2 onions, sliced
450g/1lb carrots, roughly chopped
1 tbsp garam masala
thumb-sized piece of ginger, grated
juice of 1 orange
1 litre/1¾ pints vegetable stock
200ml can reduced-fat coconut milk
410g can mixed beans, drained and
    rinsed
2 tbsp chopped coriander

1 Heat the oil in a large pan. Gently cook the onions and carrots for around 15 minutes until soft and golden. Add the garam masala and ginger, then cook for 1 minute more.

2 Add the orange juice and stock, then bring to the boil. Simmer for 10 minutes until the carrots are tender, then stir in the coconut milk. Using an electric stick blender, purée until smooth, then add the beans. Bring to a simmer, scatter over the coriander and serve.

PER SERVING 261 kcals, protein 9g, carbs 31g, fat 13g, sat fat 5g, fibre 9g, sugar 17g, salt 1.15g

Roasted onion soup with goat's cheese toasts

Roasting the onions gives the soup a rich caramelised flavour that really hits the spot on a chilly day. A perfect starter for a winter dinner party.

TAKES 1 HOUR 25 MINUTES
- **SERVES 4**

800g/1lb 12oz brown or white onions, sliced
4 tbsp olive oil
1 litre/1¾ pints vegetable stock
1 tbsp wholegrain mustard
1 tsp Marmite
handful of parsley, roughly chopped
8 thick slices bread
100g/4oz soft goat's cheese, cubed

1 Heat oven to 200C/180C fan/gas 6. Put the onions in a roasting tin with the oil and some salt and black pepper, give them a good stir, then roast for 45 minutes, stirring halfway through, until the onions are tinged brown but not burnt.

2 Tip the onions into a large pan with the stock, mustard and Marmite. Bring to the boil and simmer for 15 minutes, then stir in the parsley.

3 Toast four of the bread slices then scatter over the cheese. Ladle the soup into bowls, pop a toast into each and serve with the remaining slices of bread on the side.

PER SERVING 454 kcals, protein 15g, carbs 62g, fat 18g, sat fat 5g, fibre 6g, sugar 16g, salt 2.33g

Porcini, pancetta & spelt soup

A delicious combination of ingredients makes up this Tuscan-inspired, warming soup.
You could use bacon instead of pancetta, and if you can't find spelt, use pearl barley.

TAKES 1 HOUR ● SERVES 4

50g/2oz cubed pancetta

1 tbsp olive oil

1 bay leaf

1 onion, finely chopped

1 garlic clove, crushed

1 litre/1¾ pints vegetable stock

140g/5oz pearled spelt or farro

small handful of dried porcini
mushrooms, crumbled

2 tomatoes, skinned, deseeded and
diced

6–8 small button mushrooms,
quartered

chopped flat-leaf parsley leaves and
freshly grated Parmesan, to garnish

1 Fry the pancetta in the oil for around 2–3 minutes in a medium pan. Add the bay leaf and onion. Cook over a gentle heat until the onion is soft and translucent. Add the garlic, fry for a few seconds more, then pour over the stock and bring to the boil.

2 Rinse the spelt or farro and drain well. Add to the pan along with the porcini and tomatoes, then simmer very gently for 25–30 minutes.

3 Add the button mushrooms and simmer for 10 minutes more, or until the spelt grains are tender. Season with salt and black pepper. Ladle the soup into bowls, then sprinkle with the parsley and Parmesan.

PER SERVING 220 kcals, protein 10g, carbs 30g, fat 8g, sat fat 2g, fibre 4g, sugar 8g, salt 1.30g

Spiced parsnip soup

This parsnip soup has a warm, spicy flavour. It freezes beautifully for up to 3 months, so it is perfect for easy entertaining.

TAKES 1 HOUR 10 MINUTES

● **SERVES 6**

small knob of butter

1 onion, sliced

2 garlic cloves, sliced

thumb-sized piece of ginger, peeled and sliced

6 large parsnips, peeled and chopped

1 tsp cumin seeds

1 tsp coriander seeds

2 cardamom pods

1 tbsp garam masala

1.2 litres/2 pints vegetable stock

150ml pot double cream

TO GARNISH

1 tsp olive oil

1 tsp toasted cumin seeds

1 red chilli, deseeded and sliced

a few coriander sprigs

1 Heat the butter in a large pan. Add the onion and cook for a few minutes to soften. Throw in the garlic and ginger, cook for 1 minute more, then add the parsnips and spices. Cook for a few minutes until fragrant.

2 Pour over the vegetable stock and gently simmer for 30 minutes. Add most of the cream, bring to the boil, then turn off the heat.

3 Blitz the soup in a blender or with an electric stick blender until completely smooth. Serve in bowls, drizzled with the remaining cream and the olive oil, and scattered with cumin seeds, sliced chilli and coriander sprigs.

PER SERVING 261 kcals, protein 5g, carbs 28g, fat 15g, sat fat 7g, fibre 9g, sugar 13g, salt 0.58g

Prawn & fennel bisque

The prawn shells give a deep seafood flavour to this luxurious soup. It's quite a rich dish, so serve it in your smallest bowls. You can make and chill this a day ahead.

TAKES 1 HOUR 25 MINUTES

● **SERVES 8**

450g/1lb raw tiger prawns, shell on
4 tbsp olive oil
1 large onion, chopped
1 large fennel bulb, chopped, fronds reserved and snipped
2 carrots, chopped
150ml/¼ pint dry white wine
1 tbsp brandy
400g can chopped tomatoes
1 litre/1¾ pints fish stock
2 generous pinches of paprika
150ml pot double cream

TO SERVE

8 cooked peeled tiger prawns (leave the tail shell on for easy handling, if you like)
butter, for frying

1 Shell the prawns, then fry the shells in the oil in a large pan for about 5 minutes. Add the onion, fennel and carrots, and cook for about 10 minutes until the veg start to soften. Pour in the wine and brandy, bubble hard for about 1 minute to drive off the alcohol, then add the tomatoes, stock and paprika. Cover and simmer for 30 minutes. Meanwhile, chop the prawns.

2 Blitz the soup as finely as you can with an electric stick blender or in a food processor, then press it through a sieve into a bowl.

3 Tip into a clean pan, add the chopped prawns and cook for 10 minutes, then blitz again. Gently reheat in a pan with the cream. In another pan, fry the eight prawns in a little butter. Top the soup with the whole prawns and reserved, snipped fennel fronds.

PER SERVING 120 kcals, protein 7g, carbs 7g, fat 6g, sat fat 1g, fibre 3g, sugar 6g, salt 1.17g

Silky celeriac soup with smoked haddock

If you want to make this soup vegetarian, use vegetable rather than chicken stock. The haddock is just flaked over to finish, so you can leave it out, if you prefer.

TAKES 50 MINUTES • SERVES 6

50g/2oz unsalted butter
1 onion, chopped
1 leek, finely chopped
1 garlic bulb, cut through the middle
few thyme sprigs, plus extra leaves
    to garnish
4 bay leaves
1 celeriac, peeled and diced
2 medium potatoes, diced
1 litre/1¾ pints chicken stock
500ml/18fl oz milk
2 skinless natural smoked haddock
    fillets
500ml/18fl oz double cream

1 Heat the butter in a large pan and sweat the onion and leek with the garlic, thyme and two of the bay leaves. Add the celeriac and potatoes, and cook for 10 minutes more, stirring frequently. Pour over the stock, bring to the boil, then simmer gently for 20 minutes.

2 Meanwhile, in a deep frying pan bring the milk and remaining bay leaves to the boil. Lower to a very gentle simmer, slide in the haddock and cover with baking paper. Cook for 3–4 minutes until the fish flakes easily. Remove the fish and flake into a bowl. Cover to keep warm.

3 When the celeriac is tender, pour in the cream, bring back to the boil and remove from the heat. Remove the garlic and herb stalks, then blitz until silky smooth using an electric stick blender. Serve scattered with the flaked haddock and extra thyme leaves.

PER SERVING 636 kcals, protein 22g, carbs 16g, fat 54g, sat fat 30g, fibre 6g, sugar 9g, salt 1.87g

Rich tomato soup with pesto

When you've got rich canned tomatoes and intense, fruity sun-dries tomatoes, there's no reason not to enjoy homemade tomato soup in the depths of winter.

TAKES 25 MINUTES ● **SERVES 4**

1 tbsp butter or olive oil

2 garlic cloves, crushed

5 soft sun-dried tomatoes in oil, roughly chopped

3 × 400g cans plum tomatoes

500ml/18fl oz vegetable stock

1 tsp sugar, any type, plus more to taste (optional)

142ml pot soured cream

125g pot fresh basil pesto and a few basil leaves, to garnish

1 Heat the butter or oil in a large pan, then add the garlic and soften for a few minutes over a low heat. Add the sun-dried tomatoes, canned tomatoes, stock, sugar and seasoning, then bring to a simmer. Let the soup bubble for 10 minutes until the tomatoes have broken down a little.

2 Whizz with an electric stick blender, adding half the soured cream as you go. Taste and adjust the seasoning – add more sugar, if you need to. Serve in bowls with 1 tablespoon or so of the pesto swirled on top, a dollop of the remaining soured cream and scattered basil leaves.

PER SERVING 213 kcals, protein 8g, carbs 14g, fat 14g, sat fat 7g, fibre 4g, sugar 13g, salt 1.15g

Fresh pea & lovage soup

Lovage has a delicate, celery-like flavour, but if you can't find it, just use mint. Don't overcook the peas or they will lose their flavour and colour. Serve hot or chilled.

TAKES 30 MINUTES ● SERVES 8

about 2.5kg/5½lb fresh peas in their pods (or 900g/2lb podded or frozen peas), plus 8 whole pods to garnish
100g/4oz unsalted butter
175g/6oz spring onions, chopped
1 garlic clove, finely chopped
1.5 litres/2¾ pints vegetable stock
100g/4oz crème fraîche
bunch of lovage (about 10 sprigs), leaves picked (or use a small bunch of mint)
olive bread, thickly sliced and toasted, to serve

1 Shell the peas, leaving eight of the best-looking ones whole. Melt half the butter in a large pan and gently cook the spring onions and garlic, with the lid on, for 5 minutes without colouring. Add the stock, bring to the boil, then add the peas and eight reserved whole pods and simmer for 2–3 minutes until tender.

2 Fish out the whole pods, refresh them under cold water and reserve. Tip the crème fraîche into the soup, followed by the lovage or mint, and blitz with an electric hand blender until smooth. Season to taste. Leave to cool, then chill in the fridge, if you are serving it cold. If you're eating the soup hot, bring it to a gentle simmer but don't boil.

3 Ladle the soup into individual bowls, garnish each with a reserved whole, split pea pod and serve with a stack of toasted olive bread on the side.

PER SERVING 251 kcals, protein 9g, carbs 16g, fat 17g, sat fat 10g, fibre 7g, sugar 5g, salt 0.25g

Pumpkin soup

When puréed, pumpkin has to be one of the silkiest vegetables going. This soup has a beautiful flavour and texture. It can be frozen for up to 2 months.

TAKES 45 MINUTES • SERVES 6

2 onions, finely chopped
4 tbsp olive oil, plus extra for drizzling (optional)
1kg/2lb 4oz pumpkin, peeled, deseeded and chopped into chunks
700ml/1¼ pints vegetable or chicken stock
142ml pot double cream
4 slices wholemeal seeded bread, cut into croutons
handful of pumpkin seeds

1 Gently cook the onions in half the oil for 5 minutes until soft but not coloured. Add the pumpkin to the pan, then cook for 8–10 minutes, stirring occasionally, until it starts to soften.

2 Pour in the stock, then season. Bring to the boil, then simmer for 10 minutes until the pumpkin is very soft. Pour in the cream, bring back to the boil, then purée with an electric hand blender.

3 Heat the remaining oil in a frying pan, then fry the bread until it starts to become crisp. Add the seeds to the pan, then cook for a few minutes until they are toasted. Serve the soup scattered with croutons and seeds, and drizzled with more olive oil, if you want.

PER SERVING 317 kcals, protein 6g, carbs 20g, fat 24g, sat fat 9g, fibre 4g, sugar 6g, salt 0.54g

Squash & nigella seed soup

Nigella seeds (kalonji) are sometimes called black onion seeds; they add a peppery flavour and a crunchy texture. If you can't find them, use cumin seeds instead.

TAKES 45 MINUTES • SERVES 4

2 tbsp olive oil
1 onion, chopped
2 tsp nigella seeds
pinch of chilli powder, plus extra for
    sprinkling
800g/1lb 12oz squash, peeled,
    deseeded and cut into chunks
1 potato, peeled and cubed
850ml/1½ pints vegetable stock
small bunch of flat-leaf parsley,
    plus 4 sprigs to garnish
small queen scallops, to serve

1 Heat most of the oil in a large pan, add the onion, then fry until lightly coloured. Add the nigella seeds and a pinch of chilli powder, then fry for 1 minute. Tip in the squash, potato and stock, then bring to the boil. Stir well, cover, then simmer for 20 minutes or until the vegetables are tender.

2 Purée the soup in batches, adding a handful of parsley to each batch. Return all the soup to the pan, then gently reheat.

3 Sprinkle the queen scallops with a little chilli powder then fry them very briefly on each side in the remaining oil until lightly coloured. Pour the soup into 4 bowls and arrange the scallops in the centre with a sprig of parsley.

PER SERVING 181 kcals, protein 5g, carbs 27g, fat 7g, sat fat 1g, fibre 5g, sugar 13g, salt 0.31g

Creamy fish & mussel soup

Want to serve friends something a bit special for a Saturday lunch but don't have much time to cook? Go for this mussel soup – it's guaranteed to impress.

TAKES 25 MINUTES • SERVES 4

500g pack mussels in creamy sauce
  (find these in the chilled aisle)
1 litre/1¾ pints strong hot fish stock
500g/1lb 2oz floury potatoes, peeled
  and cut into 1cm/½in cubes
200g/8oz skinless mixed fish
small bunch of flat-leaf parsley
crusty bread, to serve

1 Drain the sauce from the mussels into a large pan and add the stock. Tip in the potatoes, cover, and bring to the boil. Once boiling, take off the lid and simmer for about 12 minutes or until the potatoes are very tender.

2 Meanwhile, cut the fish into large chunks and roughly chop the parsley. Stir the fish and mussels into the soup, then bring back to a simmer for about 3 minutes or until the fish has changed colour and flakes easily. Stir in most of the parsley. Serve scattered with the rest of the parsley and some crusty bread for mopping up the juices.

PER SERVING 185 kcals, protein 22g, carbs 8g, fat 7g, sat fat 3g, fibre 1g, sugar 1g, salt 3.45g

Watercress soup with cheesy pastries

This delicious soup makes a good light starter. Blue cheese and cashew pastry straws work well as an accompaniment – serve any leftover pastries later with drinks.

TAKES 40 MINUTES ● SERVES 6

FOR THE PASTRIES

1 sheet ready-rolled puff pastry,
  thawed (½ × 425g pack)
milk, to glaze
50g/2oz Danish blue cheese, crumbled
50g/2oz cashew nuts, finely chopped

FOR THE SOUP

1 large onion, finely chopped
25g/1oz butter
1 large potato, peeled and cubed
450ml/¾ pint milk
600ml/1 pint chicken stock
2 × 85g bags watercress

1 Heat oven to 220C/200C fan/gas 7. Unravel the pastry, brush with milk and scatter half of it with the cheese and cashews. Fold the pastry over to sandwich the nut mixture and press down firmly. Cut into 16–18 thin strips. Twist each strip a little, then lay them slightly apart on greased baking sheets. Bake for 10 minutes until golden then lift on to a wire rack to cool.

2 Fry the onion in the butter in a large pan for 5 minutes until starting to soften. Add the potato, then pour in the milk and stock. Bring to the boil then cover and lower the heat. Season and simmer for 10 minutes until the potatoes are cooked.

3 Pack the watercress into a food processor and pour over the hot potato mixture. Blend until smooth then return to the pan to reheat. Serve in small bowls or cups with the pastries on the side.

PER SERVING 321 kcals, protein 10g, carbs 27g, fat 20g, sat fat 8g, fibre 2g, sugar none, salt 1.06g

Celeriac, saffron & orange soup

A great starter – easy to make, very colourful and full of tangy flavours. It can be made in advance but make sure you prepare the gremolata fresh on the day.

TAKES ABOUT 1 HOUR • SERVES 6

FOR THE SOUP

1 large onion, chopped

2 tbsp olive oil

1 celeriac (about 600g/1lb 5oz), cut into chunks

600g/1lb 5oz potatoes, peeled and cut into chunks

1.5 litres/2¾ pints vegetable stock

1 tsp saffron strands, lightly ground in a mortar

finely grated zest and juice of 2 oranges

FOR THE GREMOLATA

1 garlic clove

1 tsp coarse sea salt

handful of flat-leaf parsley, leaves only

2 tbsp olive oil, plus extra to drizzle

1 Fry the onion in the oil in a large pan for 3–4 minutes until softened, but not coloured. Add the celeriac and potatoes. Cover and cook for 10 minutes, stirring occasionally. Stir in the stock, saffron, orange juice and half the orange zest. Bring to the boil, then simmer for around 20 minutes until the vegetables feel tender when pricked with a knife.

2 Transfer to a food processor and process until smooth (you may need to do this in batches). Return to the pan and season to taste.

3 Pound the garlic and sea salt to a paste using a pestle and mortar. Add the parsley leaves and oil, and pound to a fairly smooth paste. Reheat the soup and ladle into bowls. Spoon the gremolata on to the soup and scatter over the reserved orange zest. Serve with an extra drizzle of olive oil.

PER SERVING 209 kcals, protein 5g, carbs 24g, fat 11g, sat fat 1g, fibre 5g, sugar none, salt 1.9g

Spiced root soup with crisp spiced onions

This is a rich and earthy soup that always pleases a crowd, and the garnish of fried onion gives added texture.

TAKES ABOUT 1 HOUR • SERVES 4

2 onions
3 tbsp vegetable oil
1 tsp mustard seeds
1 tsp cumin seeds
2 leeks, sliced
3 carrots, sliced
2 medium potatoes, chopped
2 parsnips or 1 small celeriac, chopped
2–3 tsp curry paste
1.2 litres/2 pints vegetable stock
   (from granules or a cube)
250g/9oz natural yogurt
chopped coriander or parsley leaves,
   to garnish

1 Peel and halve the onions through the root, then slice thinly lengthways. Heat 2 tablespoons of the oil in a large pan, add half the onions and fry until just starting to colour. Add the mustard and cumin seeds and fry until browned.

2 Add the vegetables and curry paste, and stir until well coated. Pour in the stock and bring to the boil. Reduce the heat, and simmer for 30 minutes until the vegetables are tender. Meanwhile, heat the remaining oil in a pan and fry the remaining onions quickly until crisp. Tip on to kitchen paper to drain.

3 Purée the soup in batches, then return to the pan and stir in most of the yogurt. Reheat gently, then ladle into bowls and top each with a spoonful of the remaining yogurt, some fried onions and a scattering of coriander or parsley.

PER SERVING 240 kcals, protein 9g, carbs 25g, fat 13g, sat fat 1g, fibre 7g, sugar 16g, salt 1.45g

Spicy mussel & tomato broth

Tamarind paste has a sour–sweet flavour and is available from larger supermarkets; if you can't find it, use a drop of fresh lime juice instead.

**TAKES 25 MINUTES • SERVES 4
AS A STARTER**

1kg/2lb 4oz mussels
2 lemongrass, bruised
thumb sized-piece of galangal or ginger, sliced
2 tomatoes, chopped
5–10 small dried chillies, roasted and broken
2–3 small green chillies, sliced
1 tbsp fish sauce
1 tbsp palm or dark brown sugar
3 tbsp tamarind paste
crispy shallots, mint leaves and lime wedges, to garnish

1 Scrub and debeard the mussels, if necessary. Pour 500ml/18fl oz water into a wok or large pan and add a little salt. Add the lemongrass, galangal or ginger and tomatoes. Bring to the boil and cook for 5 minutes.

2 Tip in the mussels and the remaining ingredients, and simmer for 5 minutes or until the mussel shells open. Discard any mussels that do not open. Taste and adjust the seasoning, then garnish with the crispy shallots and mint leaves, and serve with wedges of fresh lime.

PER SERVING 105 kcals, protein 10g, carbs 13g, fat 2g, sat fat none, fibre 1g, sugar 10g, salt 1.30g

Creamy chilled basil, pea & lettuce soup

Perfect as a light starter for a summer lunch in the garden, this refreshing soup can be served in pretty cups and saucers, or even in shot glasses as a canapé.

TAKES 15 MINUTES, PLUS CHILLING
- **SERVES 4**

300g/10oz fresh or frozen peas
1 large bunch basil, leaves only
1 head soft lettuce, core removed and shredded
850ml/1½ pints cold vegetable stock
200ml pot crème fraîche

1 Cook the peas in a pan of boiling water for 3 minutes. Drain, and cool in a colander set under cold, running water.
2 Put the peas, basil, lettuce, vegetable stock and three-quarters of the crème fraîche in a blender and process until smooth. Do this in two batches. Season, cover, and chill for at least 1 hour before serving. Add a swirl of crème fraîche when serving.

PER SERVING 263 kcals, protein 8g, carbs 11g, fat 21g, sat fat 13g, fibre 4g, sugar none, salt 1g

Sweet potato & lentil soup

This soup is packed with goodness and contains three of your 5-a-day, plus it's low in fat – an all-round winner. Perfect for a Saturday lunch with friends.

TAKES 35 MINUTES ● SERVES 6

2 tsp medium curry powder
3 tbsp olive oil
2 onions, grated
1 eating apple, peeled, cored and
    grated
3 garlic cloves, crushed
20g pack coriander, stalks chopped,
    leaves left whole to garnish
thumb-sized piece of ginger, grated
800g/1lb 12oz sweet potatoes
1.2 litres/2 pints vegetable stock
100g/4oz red lentils
300ml/½ pint milk
juice of 1 lime

1 Put the curry powder into a large pan set over a medium heat and toast for 2 minutes. Add the oil, stirring as the spice sizzles in the pan. Tip in the onions, apple, garlic, coriander stalks and ginger, season, then gently cook for 5 minutes, stirring every so often.

2 Meanwhile, peel and grate the sweet potatoes. Tip into the pan with the stock, lentils, milk and seasoning, then simmer, covered, for 20 minutes. Blend until smooth using an electric stick blender. Stir in the lime juice, check the seasoning and serve topped with roughly chopped coriander leaves.

PER SERVING 287 kcals, protein 9g, carbs 49g, fat 8g, sat fat 2g, fibre 6g, sugar 17g, salt 0.71g

Fennel & almond soup

With its mildly aniseed flavour, fennel is a wonderful addition to this simple soup.
To make it more special, add some ground cardamom or a generous slug of Pernod.

TAKES 35 MINUTES ● SERVES 4

2 tbsp olive oil

1 shallot, finely chopped

2–3 fennel bulbs, trimmed and
    quartered, fronds reserved for
    garnish

2 garlic cloves, peeled

600ml/1 pint vegetable stock (from
    a cube is fine)

2 tbsp ground almonds

2 tbsp double cream

toasted baguette slices and tapenade,
    to serve

1 Heat the olive oil in a pan and cook the shallot until translucent. Add the fennel and garlic, and pour over half the stock. Bring to the boil, then simmer for about 15 minutes until the fennel is completely soft and the liquid has reduced to a sticky sauce.

2 Tip the contents of the pan into a blender along with the ground almonds and blitz until smooth. Tip back into the pan and pour over the remaining vegetable stock. Bring to the boil, then stir through the cream. Pour into bowls and sprinkle over a few fennel fronds. Serve with toasted baguette slices spread with a little tapenade.

PER SERVING 149 kcals, protein 3g, carbs 3g, fat 14g, sat fat 3g, fibre 3g, sugar none, salt 0.52g

Butternut squash soup with chilli

Give an autumn meal a warming kick. Subtlety is the key when using fresh chillies – add just enough to know it's there.

TAKES ABOUT 1 HOUR ● SERVES 4

1 butternut squash, about 1kg/2lb 4oz, peeled and deseeded
2 tbsp olive oil
1 tbsp butter
2 onions, diced
1 garlic clove, thinly sliced
2 mild red chillies, deseeded and finely chopped
850ml/1½ pints hot vegetable stock
4 tbsp crème fraîche, plus extra to swirl

1 Heat oven to 200C/180C fan/gas 6. Cut the squash into 4cm cubes, then toss in a large roasting tin with half the oil. Roast for 30 minutes, turning once during cooking, until golden and soft.

2 While the squash cooks, melt the butter with the remaining oil in a large pan, then add the onions, garlic and three-quarters of the chillies. Cover the pan and cook on a very low heat for 15–20 minutes until the onions are completely soft.

3 Tip the squash into the pan, add the stock and the crème fraîche, then whizz with an electric stick blender or blitz in a food processor until smooth. Gently reheat in the pan, then season to taste. Serve the soup in bowls with swirls of the extra crème fraîche and scattered with the remaining chopped chillies.

PER SERVING 264 kcals, protein 5g, carbs 28g, fat 15g, sat fat 7g, fibre 6g, sugar 17g, salt 0.61g

Spicy chicken & bean wrap

Perfect to pop into a lunchbox for work, school or college, this healthy snack for one is high in fibre and a good source of vitamin C. This recipe is easily doubled.

TAKES 5 MINUTES ● MAKES 1

1 large flour tortilla wrap
handful of leftover cooked chicken,
   shredded
4 tbsp drained and rinsed black beans
   or kidney beans
2 tbsp spicy salsa from a jar
4 slices pickled jalapeño chillies or
   a good splash of Tabasco sauce
3 cherry tomatoes, halved
handful of rocket or spinach leaves

1 Warm the tortilla in the microwave for 10 seconds; this will soften it and make it easier to roll.

2 Put the chicken and beans along the middle of the tortilla. Season, spoon over the salsa, then scatter with the jalapeños or Tabasco. Lay the tomatoes and rocket or spinach on top. Bring the bottom of the tortilla up over the filling. Fold the sides in, then roll it into a tight wrap. Tie the wrap up tightly to keep it together.

PER WRAP 348 kcals, protein 29g, carbs 47g, fat 6g, sat fat 1g, fibre 6g, sugar 5g, salt 1.05g

Melty onion toasts

Serve these cheese and onion toasts as a snack or a starter. The brandy is optional – if you've got some in the cupboard, it's definitely worth adding just a slug.

TAKES 55 MINUTES • MAKES 6

50g/2oz butter
6 onions, sliced
2 tsp golden caster sugar
splash of brandy (optional)
6 slices sourdough bread
300g/10oz mature Cheddar, sliced
watercress and your favourite dressing,
   to garnish

1 Heat the butter in a pan, add the onions, then sprinkle over the sugar. Sweat the onions for 20 minutes over a medium heat, stirring them occasionally, until sticky and golden. Add the brandy, if using, reduce to nothing, then season to taste.

2 Heat oven to 200C/180C fan/gas 6. Toast the bread, spread the onions over, then top with slices of cheese. Put the onion toasts on a baking sheet, then bake for 15 minutes until bubbling and golden. Serve each piece of toast on a plate with a sprig or two of dressed watercress.

PER TOAST 412 kcals, protein 17g, carbs 32g, fat 25g, sat fat 15g, fibre 3g, sugar 9g, salt 1.46g

Cheese, rosemary & potato loaf

Making a big, savoury scone loaf is a quick alternative to making bread with yeast.
You can add some bacon or ham, if you like. Best eaten just warm.

TAKES 55 MINUTES • SERVES 8

2 garlic cloves, thinly sliced
2 tbsp olive oil
350g/12oz self-raising flour, plus more
    for dusting
¼ tsp salt
1 tsp baking powder
85g/3oz cold butter, cut into cubes
150g pot natural full-fat yogurt
4 tbsp full-fat milk
250g/9oz cooked new potatoes, sliced
1 tsp chopped rosemary leaves, plus
    extra small sprigs to scatter
50g/2oz Parmesan, grated
85g/3oz Gruyère, half diced, half grated

1 Gently fry the garlic in half the oil for 10 minutes until softened. Set aside. Heat oven to 220C/200C fan/gas 7.

2 Whizz the flour, salt, baking powder and butter in a food processor. Tip into a large bowl and make a well in the middle. Warm the yogurt and milk in a pan for 1 minute; it should be hot and may go a bit lumpy looking. Tip into the flour and quickly work in using a knife.

3 Turn out the dough on to a floured surface and bring it together with floured hands, then press out to a large rectangle. Scatter over the potatoes, chopped rosemary, cooked garlic with some of its oil and most of the cheeses. Knead a few times, shape into a round, then lift on to a floured baking sheet.

4 Score the top, scatter with the remaining cheeses and the rosemary sprigs, then drizzle with the remaining oil. Bake for 25 minutes until the loaf is risen and golden.

PER SERVING 379 kcals, protein 12g, carbs 42g, fat 19g, sat fat 10g, fibre 2g, sugar 3g, salt 1.32g

Squash & ricotta wraps with coriander salsa

Try this speedy combination of sweet squash, creamy ricotta and a zingy chilli and lime salsa, all wrapped up together for a flavour-packed side dish.

TAKES 15 MINUTES • SERVES 2

½ squash, peeled, deseeded and cut into thin slices
1 tsp ground cumin
3 tbsp vegetable oil
1 green chilli, deseeded and finely chopped
handful of coriander leaves, chopped
zest and juice of 1 lime, plus extra wedges to garnish
4 soft wheat tortillas
100g/4oz ricotta

1 Toss together the squash, cumin and 2 tablespoons of the oil in a bowl, and season well. Cook the squash slices on a hot griddle for 3–5 minutes on each side until lightly charred and soft.

2 Mix together the chilli, coriander, lime zest and a squeeze of juice with the remaining oil to make a salsa. Toast the tortillas on the griddle for 30 seconds on each side. Fold them in half, then half again to make a pocket. Pop some squash slices inside and dollop over some ricotta. Drizzle with the salsa and serve straight away with lime wedges for squeezing over.

PER SERVING 549 kcals, protein 15g, carbs 64g, fat 28g, sat fat 6g, fibre 5g, sugar 13g, salt 2.68g

Rarebit toasts

Serve these tasty, cheesy toasts with a warming bowl of soup to make a substantial supper or lunch. The kids will love them.

TAKES 10 MINUTES • SERVES 8

1 sourdough loaf, sliced
200g/8oz Cheddar, grated
1 tsp Dijon mustard
2 spring onions, thinly sliced
1 egg, beaten

1 Put the bread slices under the grill and toast for 2–3 minutes until golden on one side.

2 Mix together the cheese, mustard, spring onions and egg. Spread a little over the untoasted side of each slice of bread, then pop back under the grill. Cook for 3 minutes more until the cheese is melted and golden. Serve straight away.

PER SERVING 229 kcals, protein 10g, carbs 25g, fat 10g, sat fat 6g, fibre 2g, sugar 1g, salt 1.04g

Chicken guacamole wrap

A quick and tasty treat that's ideal for lunch at home or at work. You can make it healthier by switching to a wholemeal wrap to up the fibre content.

TAKES 5 MINUTES ● MAKES 2

4 tbsp shop-bought guacamole
2 tortilla wraps
1 cooked boneless skinless chicken breast, shredded
1 red pepper, deseeded and sliced
50g/2oz Cheddar, grated

1 Spread 2 tablespoons of the guacamole down the middle of each tortilla wrap. Lay half the shredded chicken and half the sliced red pepper on top of each.
2 Sprinkle each with half of the cheese and roll up tightly. Wrap in baking parchment and tie with string, or roll tightly in cling film if you are taking the wrap to work.

PER WRAP 404 kcals, protein 31g, carbs 28g, fat 19g, sat fat 8g, fibre 3g, sugar 6g, salt 2.01g

Cheddar & bacon buns

These buns are a bit like muffins and are best served warm from the oven with lashings of butter.

TAKES 40 MINUTES ● MAKES 6

1 tsp oil, plus extra for greasing
4 rashers streaky bacon, cut into
　small pieces
50g/2oz mature Cheddar
175g/6oz plain flour
1 tsp baking powder
1 tsp English mustard
2 eggs
85g/3oz butter, melted
200ml/7fl oz milk
1 tbsp chopped parsley

1 Heat oven to 180C/160C fan/gas 4 and grease six wells of a muffin tin. Heat the oil in a frying pan and fry the bacon until crisp. Tip on to kitchen paper and allow to cool. Cut two-thirds of the cheese into little pieces, then finely grate the rest.

2 Into a bowl, sift the flour, baking powder, ½ teaspoon salt and a little black pepper. Whisk together the mustard, eggs, butter and milk in a jug. Pour the wet mix into the dry and stir a few times until just combined (the mixture will be really runny and lumpy, but don't try to stir it to make it smooth). Add the bacon, cheese pieces and parsley, being careful not to overwork the mixture.

3 Spoon into the greased wells of the muffin tin, sprinkle each with a little grated cheese, then bake for 25 minutes or until golden, risen and firm.

PER BUN 322 kcals, protein 12g, carbs 25g, fat 20g, sat fat 11g, fibre 1g, sugar 2g, salt 1.63g

10-minute steak & blue cheese wrap

A great midweek treat for steak-lovers – the blue cheese gives it a real kick. Balsamic glaze is a rich, sweet syrup made from reduced balsamic vinegar.

TAKES 10 MINUTES ● SERVES 1

1 tbsp olive oil
1 × 140g/5oz sirloin steak, trimmed
    of fat and cut into strips
1 small red onion, thinly sliced
½ red pepper, deseeded and sliced
squeeze of balsamic glaze
1 small soft flour tortilla
25g/1oz Stilton or dolcelatte
handful of rocket leaves or baby leaf
    spinach

1 Heat the oil in a hot frying pan, season the steak, then fry with the onion and pepper for 4 minutes over a moderate heat. Stir in the balsamic glaze, continue to cook for 1 minute, then remove from the heat.

2 Warm the tortilla according to the packet instructions. Slice the steak into thin strips, then tip back into the pan with any meat juices and mix with the onion and pepper. Spoon the mixture over the middle of the tortilla, crumble over the cheese, then scatter with rocket or spinach leaves. Fold to make a wrap and serve straight away.

PER SERVING 686 kcals, protein 48g, carbs 66g, fat 28g, sat fat 10g, fibre 5g, sugar 12g, salt 1.43g

Quick croque-monsieur

Need a quick, satisfying snack to keep you going? Raid the fridge and you'll soon be sitting down to a classic toasted cheese and ham favourite.

TAKES 10 MINUTES ● SERVES 2

2 slices wholemeal bread
1 egg, beaten
large handful of grated Cheddar
2 slices cooked ham, cut into strips
pinch of English mustard powder

1 Heat grill to high and toast the bread lightly on both sides. While the bread is toasting, combine all the other ingredients in a bowl.
2 Press the cheesy mix on to the slices of toast, then place under the grill for 3–4 minutes until golden and bubbling. Cut into halves and serve.

PER CROQUE-MONSIEUR 263 kcals, protein 19g, carbs 15g, fat 15g, sat fat 7g, fibre 2g, sugar none, salt 1.59g

Easy seed & grain loaf

You can choose whatever flour you like for this loaf – wholemeal, granary or white.
A thick slice is perfect with any soup.

TAKES 50 MINUTES • CUTS INTO
8 THICK SLICES

500g/1lb 2oz mixed grain flour, plus
  extra for dusting
1 tbsp each sesame and poppy seeds,
  plus extra for topping
1 sachet fast-action yeast
1 tsp salt
300ml/½ pint hand-hot water
2 tbsp olive oil, plus extra for greasing
1 tbsp clear honey

1 Tip the flour, seeds, yeast and salt into a large bowl. Mix together the water, oil and honey in a jug, then pour into the dry mix, stirring all the time to make a soft dough. If it feels sticky, sprinkle in a little more flour.

2 Turn out the dough on to a lightly floured surface and knead for 5 minutes, until it no longer feels sticky, sprinkling with more flour as you need it.

3 Oil a 1.2-litre loaf tin and put the dough in the tin, pressing it in evenly. Cover with a tea towel and leave to rise for 1 hour until it springs back when you press it with your finger. Heat oven to 200C/180C fan/gas 6.

4 Brush the loaf with water and sprinkle over the extra seeds. Bake the loaf for 30–35 minutes until it is risen and brown. Tip it out onto a wire rack to cool.

PER SLICE 277 kcals, protein 9g, carbs 45g,
fat 8g, sat fat 1g, fibre 5g, sugar 2g, salt 0.65g

Cheese & Marmite scones

This is a good way to introduce wholemeal flour into your family baking. The Marmite adds a tangy flavour to a classic favourite.

TAKES 35 MINUTES • MAKES 8

140g/5oz self-raising flour
140g/5oz wholemeal flour
1 tsp baking powder
50g/2oz cold butter, cut into small cubes, plus extra for greasing
85g/3oz mature Cheddar, grated
1 egg
1 tbsp Marmite
2 tbsp Greek or natural yogurt
3 tbsp milk, plus extra to glaze

1 Heat oven to 190C/170C fan/gas 5. Mix the flours and baking powder in a large bowl with a pinch of salt. Rub in the butter with your fingertips until the mixture resembles fine breadcrumbs (or use a food processor). Stir in half the cheese and make a well in the centre.

2 In a separate bowl, whisk together the remaining ingredients and pour into the well. With a cutlery knife, bring the mixture together to make a soft, but not sticky dough. Add a little more milk if the dough is too dry.

3 Turn out on to a floured surface, then roll out to about 2cm thick. Stamp out four scones using a round cutter, then gather the trimmings and repeat until all the dough has been used. Put on a greased baking sheet, brush with milk and scatter over the remaining cheese. Bake for 10–12 minutes until golden. Cool on a wire rack.

PER SCONE 226 kcals, protein 9g, carbs 25g, fat 11g, sat fat 6g, fibre 2g, sugar 1g, salt 0.9g

Broad bean bruschetta

Make the most of fresh broad beans while they're in the shops. This simple snack is like a posh beans on toast.

TAKES 40 MINUTES • MAKES 4

300g/10oz podded broad beans
4 tbsp olive oil, plus extra for drizzling
juice of 1 lemon
handful of mint leaves, roughly chopped
4 slices rustic white bread, such as sourdough
1 garlic clove, peeled but left whole
140g/5oz pecorino, shaved with a peeler, to garnish

1 Cook the broad beans in boiling water for 2 minutes. Drain, refresh under cold water, drain again, then peel and discard their skins.

2 Use a masher to roughly crush the beans with the oil and lemon juice, then stir through the mint. Season with salt and black pepper to taste.

3 Heat a griddle pan, toast the bread on both sides, then rub with the garlic clove. Spoon some of the beans over each slice of toasted bread, scatter over the pecorino and drizzle with more oil to serve.

PER BRUSCHETTA 429 kcals, protein 20g, carbs 32g, fat 26g, sat fat 9g, fibre 7g, sugar 2g, salt 1.18g

Scone wedges

This makes a delicious tear-and-share loaf for lunch or teatime. Top the wedges with cream cheese mixed with some chopped cucumber, spring onion and dill.

TAKES 45 MINUTES • SERVES 8

500g/1lb 2oz plain flour, plus extra
    for dusting
1 tbsp baking powder
1 tsp salt
100g/4oz cold butter
275ml/10fl oz milk
2 eggs, lightly beaten

1 Heat oven to 200C/180C fan/gas 6. Sift all the dry ingredients into a bowl. Cut the butter into small pieces and lightly rub it into the flour until the mixture resembles breadcrumbs.
2 Mix together the milk and eggs in a jug. Make a well in the centre of the flour mixture and pour in the milk and eggs. Use a knife to bring the mixture together until you have a soft dough. Turn out on to a lightly floured surface and knead for about 30 seconds until just smooth.
3 Shape into a large, round ball, about 15cm wide, then lift onto a greased baking sheet. Take a sharp knife and make four deep slashes across the scone to get eight triangular wedges. Sprinkle with a little flour, then bake for 25 minutes until risen and golden.

PER SERVING 348 kcals, protein 9g, carbs 51g, fat 13g, sat fat 7g, fibre 2g, sugar 3g, salt 1.47g

Cheesy tortillas

These tortillas are deliciously light and crispy, and they keep warm well. This sort of recipe is great for teenagers when they have to fend for themselves.

TAKES 10 MINUTES • SERVES 2–4

4 soft flour tortillas
85g/3oz Cheddar, grated
4 sun-dried tomatoes or 1 roasted red
    pepper from a jar, sliced
1 tbsp jalapeño chillies from a jar,
    drained and chopped
handful of coriander leaves, chopped
guacamole or salsa, to serve

1 Lay two tortillas side by side on a grill pan. Scatter over all of the remaining ingredients and top with the rest of the tortillas.

2 Cook under a medium grill for around 3 minutes until slightly crisp and golden. Turn, then grill the other side for about 3 minutes until the cheese has melted. Cut into wedges to serve. These tortillas are great with some guacamole or salsa served alongside.

PER SERVING (4) 248 kcals, protein 10g, carbs 34g, fat 9g, sat fat 5g, fibre 2g, sugar 1g, salt 1.03g

Spiced mackerel on toast with beetroot salsa

This heart-healthy dish is a good source of omega-3 and makes a tasty side dish.
Canned or smoked mackerel fillets will work just as well with the salad.

TAKES 15 MINUTES • SERVES 4

250g pack beetroot (not in vinegar), diced

1 eating apple, cut into wedges then thinly sliced

1 small red onion, finely sliced

juice of ½ lemon

1 tbsp olive oil, plus extra for drizzling

1 tsp cumin seeds

small bunch of coriander, leaves roughly chopped

FOR THE FISH

4 mackerel fillets, halved widthways

1 tsp mild curry powder

4 slices from a sourdough loaf or ciabatta

1 Mix together the beetroot, apple, onion, lemon juice, oil, cumin and coriander, season well, then set aside while you cook the mackerel.

2 Heat the grill to high. Put the fish onto a sheet of foil on the grill rack, sprinkle over the curry powder, drizzle with some extra oil, then season and rub the mixture into the fish. Grill for around 4–5 minutes until the skin is crisp and the fillets are cooked through; you won't need to turn over the fish.

3 Toast the bread in a toaster or alongside the fish under the grill, then drizzle with a little oil. Top with the salsa and mackerel, then pour over any pan juices and eat straight away.

PER SERVING 471 kcals, protein 25g, carbs 35g, fat 27g, sat fat 5g, fibre 3g, sugar 11g, salt 0.97g

Toasted cumin flatbreads

These flatbreads are simple to make and are a wonderful accompaniment to a bowl of soup. Made with gluten-free flour, they're ideal if you are avoiding wheat.

TAKES 20 MINUTES ● MAKES 8

400g/14oz gluten-free self-raising flour,
   plus extra for dusting
1 tbsp cumin seeds, toasted
300g/10oz natural yogurt

1 Heat the grill to medium and dust a baking sheet with a little flour. Mix together the flour and cumin seeds in a bowl, then season. Stir in the yogurt and 100ml/3½fl oz water, then mix well to form a soft dough.

2 Divide the dough into eight equal pieces, then shape them into circles or ovals about 0.5cm thick. Dust lightly with a little flour. Grill the flatbreads on the baking sheet for 3–5 minutes on each side until golden and puffed up. Serve straight away while still warm.

PER FLATBREAD 200 kcals, protein 5g, carbs 47g, fat 2g, sat fat none, fibre 1g, sugar 2g, salt 0.08g

Curried potato pasties

This spicy potato and flaky pastry combo is ideal for lunchboxes. The pasties can be stored, uncooked, in the freezer and baked from frozen for 30 minutes.

TAKES 45 MINUTES • SERVES 4

300g/10oz potatoes, peeled and cut
   into small chunks
100g/4oz frozen peas
1 onion, sliced
2 tsp vegetable oil, plus extra for
   greasing
1–2 tsp curry paste (any type)
1 tsp black mustard seeds
juice of ½ lemon
handful of coriander, chopped
375g pack ready-rolled puff pastry
flour, for dusting
1 egg, beaten, to glaze
spicy relish, to serve

1 Boil the potatoes in a pan of lightly salted water for 8 minutes until just soft. Add the peas for the last minute, drain, then set aside.

2 Fry the onion in the oil until soft. Add the curry paste and mustard seeds, then fry for a few minutes until the mixture smells fragrant. Stir in the potatoes, peas, lemon juice and coriander; leave to cool.

3 Heat oven to 200C/180C fan/gas 6. Unroll the pastry on a floured surface with the long side towards you, then roll it out a little more to make a square shape. Cut into four squares, then cut each in half so you have eight long rectangles. Put four of the rectangles on to a greased baking sheet, brush the edges with egg and put a quarter of the filling down the centre. Top with the remaining pastry rectangles, then pinch the edges together to seal. Brush with egg, then bake the pasties for around 20 minutes. Serve with a spicy relish.

PER PASTY 480 kcals, protein 11g, carbs 53g, fat 26g, sat fat 10g, fibre 3g, sugar 4g, salt 0.86g

Spiced courgette fritters

These are similar to Indian pakoras. The fritters need to be cooked at the last minute, but the batter can be made an hour in advance.

**TAKES 50 MINUTES ● SERVES 4
(MAKES 8–12 FRITTERS)**

FOR THE FRITTERS

3 courgettes, finely sliced

1 large onion, halved and finely sliced

1 red chilli, halved, deseeded and finely
sliced

1 tbsp garam masala

1 tsp ground turmeric

handful of coriander leaves, roughly
chopped

140g/5oz self-raising flour

½ tsp bicarbonate of soda

sunflower oil, for frying

FOR THE TOMATO SALSA

2 tomatoes, finely chopped

1 small red onion, finely chopped

1 green chilli, finely chopped (optional)

1 tsp tomato ketchup

1 Tip all the fritter ingredients into a bowl. Gradually work in about 200ml/7fl oz cold water until everything is bound in a thick, spoonable batter. Heat a decent layer of oil in a large frying pan, then fry large spoonfuls of the batter for 2 minutes until golden. Flip them over, cook on the other side, then lift on to kitchen paper and keep warm while you cook another batch.

2 Make the salsa by mixing together all the ingredients. Serve the fritters with the salsa for spooning over.

PER SERVING 355 kcals, protein 7g, carbs 38g, fat 21g, sat fat 3g, fibre 3g, sugar 8g, salt 0.59g

Full English kebabs

If the sun is shining you can easily cook these kebabs on the barbecue, just add a few minutes to the cooking time to ensure the sausages are cooked all the way through.

TAKES 20 MINUTES ● SERVES 4

1 tbsp olive oil
1 tbsp clear honey
1 tbsp wholegrain mustard
8 rashers streaky bacon, snipped in half
8 chipolata sausages, snipped in half
16 button or chestnut mushrooms
16 cherry tomatoes
4 small crusty baguettes or rolls, salad leaves and tomato or brown sauce, to serve

1 Heat grill to high. Mix together the oil, honey and mustard with some seasoning in a small bowl and set aside.
2 Wrap a piece of bacon around each half sausage, then start to load up the four kebabs. On each skewer thread a mushroom, a bacon-wrapped sausage chunk and a cherry tomato, then repeat so there are two of each on each skewer.
3 Brush the honey–mustard sauce over the skewers, then grill, turning, for 10 minutes until the sausages are golden, sticky and cooked through. Split the rolls, and serve alongside the skewers with salad leaves and a dollop of tomato or brown sauce per person.

PER SERVING 282 kcals, protein 15g, carbs 7g, fat 21g, sat fat 7g, fibre 1g, sugar 5g, salt 2.05g

Summer sausage rolls

Always a popular favourite, here's a new style of sausage roll filled with tasty chicken, bacon and sun-dried tomatoes. Perfect for a snack or picnic.

TAKES 40 MINUTES • MAKES 20

2 large boneless skinless chicken
    breasts, chopped
1 garlic clove, crushed
3 rashers streaky bacon, thinly sliced
4 sun-dried tomatoes, chopped
handful of basil leaves, chopped
375g pack ready-rolled puff pastry
flour, for dusting
1 egg yolk, beaten, to glaze
25g/1oz sesame seeds, to sprinkle

1 Whizz the chicken and garlic in a food processor until the chicken is minced. Tip in the bacon, sun-dried tomatoes and basil. Pulse for 5 seconds to just mix through. Season well.

2 Roll the pastry sheet on a floured surface and cut in half lengthways. Spread half the chicken mixture along the middle of one of the pastry strips, then roll over the pastry to cover, pinching the ends together to seal. Using a sharp knife, cut into 2.5cm long pieces. Repeat with the remaining pastry strip.

3 Heat oven to 200C/180C fan/gas 6. Put the rolls on a large baking sheet. Brush with the egg, then sprinkle with seeds. Bake for 20 minutes until golden.

PER ROLL 119 kcals, protein 6g, carbs 6g, fat 8g, sat fat 3g, fibre 1g, sugar none, salt 0.38g

Bean dip with veggie sticks

If you're taking this snack to work, wrap the vegetable sticks in a damp piece of kitchen paper to stop them losing their crunch. This recipe contains all of your 5-a-day.

TAKES 10 MINUTES • SERVES 1

215g can butter beans, drained
squeeze of lemon juice
1 small garlic clove, crushed
1 tbsp chopped parsley leaves
1 tbsp chopped mint leaves
2 tsp olive oil
1 celery stick
1 carrot
½ red pepper, deseeded

1 Whizz the drained butter beans in a food processor with the lemon juice, garlic, chopped parsley and mint, oil and 1 tablespoon water.
2 Trim and slice the celery into sticks. Peel and cut the carrot into sticks and slice the red pepper. Serve the bean dip with the vegetable dippers.

PER SERVING 253 kcals, protein 10g, carbs 34g, fat 10g, sat fat 1g, fibre 11g, sugar 17g, salt 0.3g

Sweet potatoes with mushrooms & rosemary

Ring the changes and try jacket sweet potatoes. If you prefer to fully oven-bake them rather than microwaving, cook for 40–50 minutes, turning halfway through.

TAKES 30 MINUTES ● SERVES 2

2 sweet potatoes, about 300g/10oz
   each
1 tbsp olive oil
200g/8oz chestnut mushrooms, halved
1 tsp chopped rosemary leaves or
   ½ tsp dried
2 tbsp freshly grated Parmesan, to
   sprinkle

1 Heat oven to 200C/180C fan/gas 6. Prick the potatoes several times with a fork, then microwave on High for 8–10 minutes, turning once, until tender. Meanwhile, heat the oil in a non-stick pan, add the mushrooms and rosemary, and cook over a fairly high heat, stirring, until the mushrooms are tender and lightly coloured. Season to taste.

2 Put the potatoes on a baking sheet and roast in the oven for 15 minutes until the skins start to crisp. Split open and spoon over the mushrooms. Sprinkle with Parmesan to serve.

PER SERVING 359 kcals, protein 8g, carbs 65g, fat 9g, sat fat 3g, fibre 8g, sugar 17g, salt 0.47g

Baked garlic mushrooms

Need a quick food fix? Try these tasty garlic mushrooms served on crispy toast for a light, yet satisfying snack.

TAKES 20 MINUTES • SERVES 1

4 large portobello mushrooms
olive oil, to grease and drizzle
2 garlic cloves, finely chopped
2 slices bread
1 tsp chopped parsley leaves and a
few toasted pine nuts, to garnish

1 Heat oven to 200C/180C fan/gas 6. Put the mushrooms on a lightly oiled baking sheet. Drizzle with oil, sprinkle with garlic, then season. Bake for 15 minutes until tender.
2 Toast the bread on both sides. Put the mushrooms on the toast, then sprinkle with the chopped parsley and toasted pine nuts.

PER SERVING 468 kcals, protein 13g, carbs 37g, fat 30g, sat fat 5g, fibre 5g, sugar 3g, salt 0.93g

Hot corncakes with avocado, bacon & basil

Corncakes like these are classic brunch food in Australia. They're also delicious made with shredded chicken and lots of fresh coriander.

TAKES 20 MINUTES ● SERVES 4

2 tbsp olive oil, plus extra, if required, for greasing

1 red pepper, deseeded and diced

1 red or green chilli, deseeded and chopped

50g/2oz self-raising flour

1 egg, beaten

3 tbsp milk

2 × 330g cans sweetcorn niblets, drained

handful of basil leaves, chopped, plus extra to garnish

8 rashers streaky or back bacon

juice of ½ lemon

1 or 2 avocados, peeled, stoned and sliced

1 Heat grill to high. Heat 1 tablespoon of the oil in a large non-stick frying pan and sizzle the pepper for 5 minutes until softened, adding the chopped chilli for the final minute.

2 Put the flour into a large bowl, make a well, and stir in the egg and then the milk to make a batter. Stir in the corn and chopped basil, then season well.

3 Add more oil to the pan, if you need to, then drop in tablespoons of the batter. Cook for 2 minutes until risen and golden underneath, then cook for just 1 minute more. You'll need to do these in batches to make 12 in total. Keep warm while you cook the rest.

4 Meanwhile, grill the bacon. Mix the lemon juice and remaining tablespoon of oil together with some seasoning. Serve three cakes each, topped with the avocado, bacon, basil leaves and a drizzle of the dressing.

PER SERVING 420 kcals, protein 16g, carbs 49g, fat 19g, sat fat 4g, fibre 4g, sugar 16g, salt 2.49g

Houmous-topped avocado with tomato salad

On a summer's day what could be better than this light, tasty salad on top of a good-for-you avocado?

TAKES 15 MINUTES • SERVES 2
½ small red onion, sliced
2 tomatoes, chopped
handful of pitted olives, halved
squeeze of fresh lemon juice
olive oil, for drizzling
1 avocado
4 tbsp houmous
4 slices ciabatta, toasted, to serve

1 Mix the red onion with the chopped tomatoes, olives, a squeeze of lemon juice and a drizzle of olive oil to make the salad.
2 Halve and stone the avocado, and put each half on to a plate. Divide the houmous between the avocado halves, spooning it into the space where the stone was, then scatter over the tomato salad. Drizzle with a little more oil, then serve with toasted ciabatta.

PER SERVING 527 kcals, protein 11g, carbs 39g, fat 38g, sat fat 5g, fibre 8g, sugar 7g, salt 1.42g

Hash browns with mustard & smoked salmon

These golden hash browns are also delicious topped with a poached egg. For a healthier version, use a spray of oil when frying them.

TAKES 20 MINUTES • SERVES 4

1 large potato (about 350g/12oz), washed
1 tbsp plain flour
1 tbsp wholegrain mustard or horseradish sauce
knob of butter
1 tbsp sunflower oil
4 slices smoked salmon
soured cream or crème fraîche and chives, to garnish

1 Grate the unpeeled potato on to a clean tea towel. Bring up the edges of the towel, then squeeze over the sink to remove any excess water in the potatoes. Tip into a bowl and add the flour and mustard or horseradish. Season well and mix together.

2 Divide the mixture into eight balls and flatten between your hands. Heat the butter and oil in a large frying pan then add the potatoes. Cook the hash browns for 2–3 minutes on each side, over a medium heat, until golden.

3 Stack a couple of hash browns on each serving plate and top with a slice of smoked salmon, a dollop of soured cream or crème fraîche and a garnish of chives to serve.

PER SERVING 153 kcals, protein 9g, carbs 18g, fat 6g, sat fat 2g, fibre 1g, sugar 1g, salt 1.61g

Baked pitta bread & houmous

Dips and crisps are always popular with kids – here's a healthier version: a wholesome dip served with baked pitta 'crisps'.

TAKES 20 MINUTES ● SERVES 4

6 mini pitta breads, split in half, then cut into 2

2 tbsp olive oil

¼ tsp sea salt

FOR THE HOUMOUS

410g can chickpeas, drained and rinsed

juice of 2 lemons

2 garlic cloves, crushed

2 tbsp olive oil

¼ tsp sea salt

150ml/¼ pint tahini paste

1 Heat oven to 200C/180C fan/gas 6. Spread the pitta pieces over the base of a large roasting tin. Drizzle with the oil and sprinkle with the sea salt. Bake for 6 minutes until just beginning to brown and become crispy. Serve warm or cold – they will keep in an airtight container for up to 4 days.

2 To make the houmous, whizz together the chickpeas, lemon juice, garlic, olive oil, sea salt and tahini paste in a food processor until just smooth. Loosen with a little water, if needed, and serve with the pitta crisps.

PER SERVING 307 kcals, protein 10g, carbs 40g, fat 14g, sat fat 2g, fibre 4g, sugar 2g, salt 1.24g

Smoked mackerel dip

Make a batch of this healthy dip and keep it in the fridge for whenever you want a snack. You can make it with other kinds of smoked fish, or even drained canned tuna.

TAKES 10 MINUTES ● SERVES 2

250g smoked mackerel fillets, skinned and finely flaked

142ml pot soured cream

bunch of spring onions, trimmed and finely chopped

4 tsp horseradish sauce

selection of crunchy raw vegetables, such as carrots, pepper, celery and courgettes, to serve

1 In a mixing bowl, stir together the smoked mackerel, soured cream and spring onions to make a textured dip, then stir in the horseradish. Spoon into a serving bowl.

2 Trim and slice the vegetables into sticks and serve with the dip. The dip can be stored, covered, in the fridge for up to 3 days.

PER SERVING 561 kcals, protein 25g, carbs 5g, fat 49g, sat fat 17g, fibre 1g, sugar 5g, salt 2.23g

Grilled mushrooms with goat's cheese

Goat's cheese and ham turn meaty portobello mushrooms into a satisfying lunch.
Serve with a winter leaf salad with an orange and oil dressing.

TAKES 20 MINUTES • SERVES 4

8 large portobello mushrooms
2 garlic cloves, finely chopped
150g pack mild goat's cheese
4 slices cooked ham, halved
2 tbsp olive oil
50g/2oz pine nuts, lightly toasted
small handful of parsley, roughly
　　chopped
toasted ciabatta and dressed winter
　　leaf salad, to serve

1 Heat oven to 200C/180C fan/gas 6. Wipe the mushrooms with kitchen paper and put on a baking sheet, gills facing up. Season, then scatter with the garlic, dot with the goat's cheese and top each with a piece of ham.

2 Drizzle over the oil, cover with foil, then cook in the oven for 10 minutes. After 5 minutes, remove the foil and return to the oven.

3 When the mushrooms are tender and the cheese is melted and bubbling, scatter over the pine nuts and parsley. Serve with toasted ciabatta and a dressed winter leaf salad.

PER SERVING 257 kcals, protein 14g, carbs 2g, fat 22g, sat fat 6g, fibre 2g, sugar 2g, salt 1.12g

Summer nachos with prawns

If you want to make this simple lunch veggie, just replace the prawns with a sliced
avocado tossed in a little lime juice to stop it discolouring.

TAKES 5 MINUTES ● SERVES 2

200g bag spicy or cool tortilla chips
small bunch of coriander, roughly
    chopped
142ml pot soured cream or reduced-fat
    crème fraîche
1 lime, cut into quarters
2–3 tomatoes, cut into chunks
3 spring onions, sliced
200g bag cooked peeled prawns,
    defrosted and drained
sliced jalapeño chillies from a jar
    (optional)

1 Spread the tortilla chips over a large
plate. Stir most of the coriander through
the soured cream or crème fraîche,
squeeze in the juice of one lime quarter
and season to taste.

2 Spoon this mixture over the tortilla
chips, then scatter over the rest of the
ingredients with the chillies, if using, and
the remaining coriander. Serve at once.

PER SERVING 722 kcals, protein 33g, carbs 66g,
fat 38g, sat fat 9g, fibre 7g, sugar 7g, salt 4.32g

Smoked salmon layer

This no-cook midday snack is quickly put together and can easily be doubled or trebled. If you're not keen on smoked salmon, use slices of cooked ham instead.

TAKES 10 MINUTES ● SERVES 1

½ carrot, peeled
2 radishes, trimmed
small chunk of cucumber, deseeded
3 tbsp full-fat soft cheese
juice of ½ lemon or lime
small handful of coriander leaves,
    roughly chopped
2 slices smoked salmon
drizzle of olive oil, to garnish
bread and butter, to serve

1 Grate the carrot, radishes and cucumber. Mix in the cheese, lemon or lime juice and most of the coriander, then season with salt and pepper to taste.
2 Lay a slice of salmon on a plate, top with the vegetable mix, then drape over the other slice of salmon. Scatter with the remaining coriander, drizzle with oil and serve with bread and butter.

PER SERVING 231 kcals, protein 16g, carbs 6g, fat 16g, sat fat 8g, fibre 1g, sugar 5g, salt 2.88g

Brie bruschetta with tomato, herbs & Serrano ham

Bored with sandwiches? These tasty bruschetta make a great summertime lunch.

TAKES 40 MINUTES • SERVES 4

2 tbsp olive oil
2 shallots, finely chopped
125ml/4fl oz double cream
small bunch of chives, snipped
4 thick slices white bloomer-style
  bread
2 tomatoes, sliced
10–12 slices Brie or Camembert
4 slices Serrano ham or prosciutto
rocket leaves, to garnish

1 Heat 1 teaspoon of the oil in a pan and gently cook the shallots for 2 minutes until soft but not coloured. Pour in the cream, bring to a simmer, then reduce it by about half. The cream will look like a thick sauce at this point. Stir in the snipped chives.

2 Heat grill to high. Brush the remaining oil over the bread and grill on both sides until toasted. Top each slice with some tomato, then cheese, then Serrano ham or prosciutto, and finally spread over about 1 tablespoon of the thickened cream to cover the ham. Put back under the hot grill until the cream starts to colour and glaze, and the cheese has begun to melt. Serve with rocket leaves scattered over the top.

PER SERVING 506 kcals, protein 19g, carbs 28g, fat 36g, sat fat 18g, fibre 1g, sugar 4g, salt 1.8g

Turkey meatball wraps

If you like a char-grilled flavour to your tortillas, heat them in a very hot, dry frying pan for 1 minute until warm and toasty.

TAKES 20 MINUTES ● SERVES 4

500g pack minced turkey
1 tsp each ground cumin and coriander
1 onion, finely chopped
1 tbsp sunflower oil
8 tortillas
200g bag crunchy salad leaves
150g pot 0% fat Greek yogurt

1 Tip the turkey, spices, onion and some salt and black pepper into a bowl, and mix well with a fork or your hands. Shape into 16 meatballs and flatten slightly (this makes them easier to cook). Heat the oil in a non-stick frying pan, then fry the meatballs for 8–10 minutes until browned and cooked through.

2 Meanwhile, warm the tortillas in the microwave on High for 1 minute. Spread with salad, then add two meatballs and a little yogurt to each tortilla and roll up. Serve two wraps per person.

PER SERVING 370 kcals, protein 39g, carbs 37g, fat 9g, sat fat 1g, fibre 3g, sugar 5g, salt 1.15g

Index

almond & fennel soup 142–3
asparagus soup, classic 24–5
avocado
  bacon, basil, & hot corncakes
    192–3
  houmous-topped 194–5
  salsa 18–19

bacon
  & Cheddar buns 158–9
  & pea chowder 62–3
  barley & wild mushroom broth
    48–9
  basil, avocado & hot corncakes
    192–3
  full English kebabs 182–3
  leek & rosemary soup 30–1
  potato & cabbage soup 36–7
  potato & leek soup 82–3
  summer sausage rolls 184–5
barley
  chickpea & leek soup 98–9
  mushroom & bacon broth 48–9
beans
  & chicken spicy wrap 146–7
  broad, bruschetta 168–9
  dip, & veggie sticks 186–7
  kidney, spiced soup 92–3
  spiced citrus soup 108–9
  spicy soup 18–19
  Tuscan soup 96–7
  white, & pesto pot 40–1
beetroot salsa 174–5
bisque, prawn & fennel 116–17
broth

hearty ham & cabbage 66–7
kale & chorizo 80–1
mussel & tomato spicy 136–7
wild mushroom, bacon &
  barley 48–9
bruschetta
  Brie, tomato, herbs & ham
    208–9
  broad bean 168–9
buns, Cheddar & bacon 158–9
butter, lime 26–7

cabbage
  & hearty ham broth 66–7
  Savoy, potato & bacon soup
    36–7
carrot
  & lentil spiced soup 42–3
  spiced soup 86–7
cauliflower cheese soup 102–3
celeriac
  & haddock soup 118–19
  saffron & orange soup 132–3
cheese
  & Marmite scones 166–7
  blue, & steak wrap 160–1
  cauliflower, soup 102–3
  Cheddar & bacon buns 158–9
  cheesy pastries 130–1
  cheesy tortillas 172–3
  croque monsieur 162–3
  rarebit toasts 154–5
  rosemary & potato loaf 150–1
  see also Brie; ricotta
chestnut & mushroom soup

  104–5
chicken
  & bean spicy wrap 146–7
  & lentil spiced soup 50–1
  & watercress soup 70–1
  easy noodle soup 60–1
  guacamole wrap 156–7
  lentil & sweetcorn chowder
    44–5
  noodle soup 58–9
  summer sausage rolls 184–5
chickpea
  & sweet potato soup 14–15
  chilli & red lentil soup 76–7
  leek & barley soup 98–9
  soup 26–7
chilli
  & squash soup 144–5
  lentil & chickpea soup 76–7
chowder
  pea & bacon 62–3
  smoked haddock 10
coconut
  & prawn laksa 16–17
  & sweet potato soup 22–3
  noodle spicy soup 20–1
consommé, raviolini & rosemary
  54–5
coriander salsa 152–3
courgette(s)
  15-minute summer soup 68–9
  spiced fritters 180–1
couscous, & veg soup 94–5
croque monsieur, quick 162–3
cucumber & yogurt soup 32–3

cumin flatbreads, toasted 176–7
curried potato pasties 178–9

dips
  bean 186–7
  smoked mackerel 200–1

fennel
  & almond soup 142–3
  & prawn bisque 116–17
fish & mussel soup 128–9
flatbreads, toasted cumin 176–7
fritters, spiced courgette 180–1

gammon & spring greens soup
  100–1
garlic mushrooms, baked 190–1
goat's cheese
  & grilled mushrooms 202–3
  toasts 110–11
gremolata 132–3
guacamole chicken wrap 156–7

haddock
  & sweetcorn soup 64–5
  smoked, & celeriac soup
    118–19
  smoked, chowder 10
ham
  & cabbage hearty broth 66–7
  quick croque monsieur 162–3
  Serrano, tomato, herbs & Brie
    bruschetta 208–9
hash browns, mustard & smoked
  salmon 196–7
houmous
  & baked pitta bread 198–9
  -topped avocado 194–5

kale & chorizo broth 80–1
kebabs, full English 182–3

laksa, prawn & coconut 16–17
leek
  bacon & potato soup 82–3
  bacon & rosemary soup 30–1
  barley & chickpea soup 98–9
lentil(s)
  & carrot spiced soup 42–3
  & chicken spiced soup 50–1
  & sweet potato soup 140–1
  red, chickpea & chilli soup 76–7
  sweetcorn & chicken chowder
    44–5
lettuce, basil & pea soup 138–9
lime butter 26–7
loaves
  cheese, rosemary & potato
    150–1
  easy seed & grain 164–5
lovage & pea fresh soup 122–3

mackerel
  smoked, dip 200–1
  spiced, on toast 174–5
Marmite & cheese scones 166–7
meatballs, turkey, wraps 210–11
minestrone, chunky 56–7
mushroom(s)
  & chestnut soup 104–5
  baked garlic 190–1
  grilled, & goat's cheese 202–3
  hearty soup 72–3
  rosemary & sweet potato
    188–9
  wild, bacon & barley broth
    48–9
  wild, cream of, soup 84–5

  see also porcini
mussel
  & fish creamy soup 128–9
  & tomato spicy broth 136–7

nachos, summer 204–5
nigella & squash soup 126–7
noodle soup
  chicken 58–9
  coconut spicy 20–1
  easy 60–1
  hot & sour Thai 52–3
  tom yam 88–9

onion(s)
  crisp spiced 134–5
  melty toasts 148–9
  roasted, & goat's cheese toasts
    110–11
orange, celeriac & saffron soup
  132–3

pancetta, spelt & porcini soup
  112–13
parsnip, spiced soup 114–15
pasta spicy soup 106–7
pasties, curried potato 178–9
pastries, cheesy 130–1
pea
  15-minute summer soup 68–9
  & bacon chowder 62–3
  & lovage fresh soup 122–3
  & watercress soup 12–13
  lettuce & basil soup 138–9
  minted soup 28–9
pepper, smoky, & sweetcorn
chowder 90–1
pesto
  & rich tomato soup 120–1

& white bean pot 40–1
pitta bread, baked, & houmous
198–9
porcini, pancetta & spelt soup
112–13
potato
cabbage & bacon soup 36–7
cheese & rosemary loaf 150–1
curried pasties 178–9
leek & bacon soup 82–3
mashed, & prawn chowder
46–7
prawn
& coconut laksa 16–17
& fennel bisque 116–17
& mashed potato chowder
46–7
spicy soup 38–9
with summer nachos 204–5
pumpkin soup 124–5

raviolini & rosemary consommé
54–5
ricotta & squash wraps with
coriander salsa 152–3
root soup, spiced 134–5
rosemary
& raviolini consommé 54–5
bacon & leek soup 30–1
potato & cheese loaf 150–1
sweet potato & mushrooms
188–9

saffron, orange & celeriac soup
132–3
salads
Asian 86–7
tomato 194–5
salmon

smoked, & mustard 196–7
smoked, layer 206–7
salsa
avocado 18–19
beetroot 174–5
coriander 152–3
soup 74–5
tomato 180–1
sausage
full English kebabs 182–3
Polish, soup 78–9
sausage rolls, summer 184–5
scones
cheese & Marmite 166–7
scone wedges 170–1
spelt, porcini & pancetta soup
112–13
spring greens & gammon soup
100–1
squash
& nigella seed soup 126–7
& ricotta wraps 152–3
soup with chilli 144–5
steak, & blue cheese wrap 160–1
sweet potato
& chickpea soup 14–15
& lentil soup 140–1
mushroom & rosemary 188–9
speedy soup 22–3
sweetcorn
& haddock soup 64–5
& pepper chowder 90–1
chicken & lentil chowder 44–5
hot corncakes 192–3

toast(s)
cumin flatbreads 176–7
goat's cheese 110–11
melty onion 148–9

rarebit 154–5
spiced mackerel & beetroot
salsa 174–5
tomato
& mussel spicy broth 136–7
herbs, ham & Brie bruschetta
208–9
rich soup & pesto 120–1
salad 194–5
salsa 180–1
tortillas, cheesy 172–3
turkey meatball wraps 210–11

veg soup
Moroccan 94–5
versatile 34–5
veggie sticks & bean dip 186–7

watercress
15-minute summer soup 68–9
& chicken soup 70–1
& pea soup 12–13
soup, & cheese pastries 130–1
wraps
chicken & bean spicy 146–7
chicken guacamole 156–7
squash & ricotta 152–3
steak & blue cheese 160–1
turkey meatball 210–11

yogurt & cucumber soup 32–3